In Leaf

Rosalía de Castro

A Transfoliation
–polyfabulation–
by
Erín Moure
from her 2016 translation of
Rosalía de Castro's *New Leaves*

for her readers and friends

First Printing October 2019 (small corrections Nov 5, 2019)
IBSN: 978-0-9867595-4-3

Published by:

Zat-So Productions

flies in the face of reason

Cover photo @Erín Moure: Rita Wong, Canadian poet and water protector who like Rosalía de Castro struggles for "the people who are missing," up on the hills at Grand Haven above the mighty Peace, 2018. Rita was sentenced by Canadian courts to 28 days in jail in August 2019 for participating in a peaceful protest in B.C. against oil pipeline construction. Her courage!

Photo page 3: Maria Cardarelly (photo held by RAG, in public domain).

AGRADECEMENTOS

With thanks to Anxo Angueira, María do Cebreiro, Helena Miguélez Carballeira, Maria Reimóndez, and Olga Castro for their vital work on Rosalía de Castro, which makes my own work possible. And to Chus Pato, who encourages me, and Belén Martín Lucas, whose friendship and support and feminist intelligence makes her forever my *xemelga*. And to POEM, for publishing a poem, and to Cheryl Emerson, for reading the draft book. It remains that I am the sole person responsible for any errors.

In Leaf

Rosalía de Castro

Zat-So Productions

flies in the face of reason

translated by Erín Moure

ONE ART.

*[...]Artists can only invoke a people, their need for one goes to the very heart of what they're doing, it's not their job to create one, and they can't. Art is resistance: it resists death, slavery, infamy, shame. But a people can't worry about art. How is a people created, through what terrible suffering? When a people's created, it's through its own resources, but in a way that links up with something in art or links art to what it lacked. . [...] **Gilles Deleuze to Antonio Negri, 1990.[1]***

Poetry is the taste of thinking in the mouth.

My own psyche, as child and grandchild of Europeans driven to North American shores by wars and poverty, by loss and hope for futures, insists that I resist the demonization of migrants fleeing for centres of economic stability where it may be possible to rebuild lives. As did Rosalía de Castro in *her* time, I see the economic forces today as complex and wounding, and am alarmed at the harms as resulting from the concentration of capital in the hands of the few, and from the accelerating effects—already noted by Rosalía 150 years ago—of climate change and ecological degradation in the name of profit and Western comfort. Today, people are on the move in ever greater numbers away from long-term homes, giving rise to border clashes, walls, wars, unemployment, gig uncertainty, and to abuses of women, particularly Indigenous women, and of the vulnerable (disabled, elderly, children).

Rosalía de Castro, today, is my contemporary. In facing such forces, her ire and insistence on women's thinking and on mental health ring clear. She recognized in the 19th century that precarity causes forced migration. In her poems, the historic migrancy of Galicians speaks not just in the old Spanish currency of *real* or *peseta*, but in the contemporary currency of the euro and dollar. And it speaks to and with women, and all those living in precarity, or subject to social violence or exclusion.

It's this Rosalía de Castro I wish to share.

Erín Moure
Montréal, October 2019

---

[1] *Futur Antérieur* (Spring 1990), tr. Martin Joughin. http://www.generation-online.org/p/fpdeleuze3.htm.

(eye/Hnad)

What intrigues in *Follas Novas* is the Galician language (says
Wikipedia), that the poetry of intimacy be in Galician. If this is true,
then what is of interest in the book when Galician is removed from it?

I would maintain that the eye/hand coordination of the translator lays
bare a"view" of the Galician language itself, though its patterns and
surfaces are made over into the other (target) medium, English.

Brush, movement, spatter, solicitude all must be visible in the English
as ripples or rhythms...

The interferences of the translator—such as this note—must be wrought
ever more visibly in the book, I think, and the implications of the
poems, their residual resonance, articulated not simply in the poems
but alongside them (translated normally, normatively)

To shine light upon a process of thinking... visible:
a movement... visible:
thought's movement on the surface leaving Rosalía intact or

the eye
the surface of language piercing this eye...,

(caught, as we are... in the...
torpour of history)

This book is gratefully dedicated to the Board and members of the Sociedade de Beneficencia dos Naturales de Galicia na Habana—*one of the most glorious and respected achievements of Galicians in Havana—on the anniversary of its founding.*

Rosalía Castro de Murguía
Honorary member
Santiago de Compostela, Galicia 23 February 1880

translated from Galician

For a long time I couldn't even imagine publishing these poems; I'd set them aside. But to stay alive as a writer also means sending poems to print. Poems themselves are mute; they are not yet literature. They don't exist until they have a reader, as my translator says. I could have never have predicted they'd end up where they are today, in these versions of my versions, with you readers in the present, in English, when I myself am beyond destination.

The contradictions of life and health in the late 19th century meant that I set these poems aside for a decade after writing them. Urged to pick them up again, I found in them simply a sad book with no merit. They were written in exile, illness and absence: in the dry plains of Castile, far from verdant and mountainous Galicia. They reflect my state of mind then and, perhaps, my capacity as a woman (or so they say) for feeling the pain of others. What if sadness is the muse of our time? It knows me well; it claims me as its own and I can't shake it off. It's part of the heart muscle. *Epigenetic markers, as they now say.* How can one person's experience possibly speak beyond its own singularity? *It's a question that stops a woman. Did Keats ask that question? I think not. Did Homer? I doubt it. I don't think Derrida asked it either.* Yet I don't think myself inspired, or that I've written a book that transcends my own situation. No, that was not my aim. Though many serious matters need speaking in poetry, even a century and a half after I wrote my own poems, women are still too often seen as frail, able only to speak of imagination and feeling. To publish my poems, in 1880, I had to feign to agree, *but really, in 2019?* It is as if from the eternal honeycomb of women's inner lives, honey emerges, sweet or fragrant, but honey just the same, nothing more. If the issues occupying the great minds of men concern women, it's when they bring sorrow home. It's our job to see to their wounds, offer help and support, more with acts than with words.

---

[2] In a rhetorical posing between her poems and the prejudices of her time, de Castro reflects not just on the provenance of the poems (of which she doesn't tell the whole truth), but on the condition of women and their relationship to thinking. When she claims women's role is light and their thought frivolous, she's got tongue in cheek! In the very first book of poems, "Vagaries" ("Whimsies," if you like, or "Extravagances"), she makes clear that thinking is her business. *Angueira, too, discusses this: 354-356.*

As if we were butterflies who alight from rose to rose, the hard work of thinking is not ours. We weaken thinking by even trying; our frivolous spirits so easily stray. *Sound familiar? What a way to look at butterflies!* Beneath the flow of forms, men of study tend to leave women out, as if there's naught in our thoughts but an insubstantial froth of vulgarities. Art requires speculation and in this speculative thinking, vulgarity is not helpful.[3] To avoid such momentous sins, I stick with poetry, though even there I can encounter a felicitous expression or chance idea, an unutterable force that pierces flesh like an arrow, makes it shudder, and resonates as if responding to our sighs as we grapple with earthly sorrow.

This book is no sequel to *Galician Songs*. Written amid family and health upheavals, it has not the innocence of first impressions. The sun of life that illuminates our world at dawn glows differently at sunset, shrouded in clouds announcing autumn.

Galicia, the soul of *Songs*, is here less directly visible. *Galicia, as my translator says, could be many places.* If only death is able to free the spirit from its shroud of flesh, we poets are the undead: we can't release ourselves from the world that shrouds us, or stop echoing the cries that persist in every mouth. Though I can't say what in my book arises from my troubles, and what from those of others, I take full responsibility. In this book, I give priority to poems that express the tribulations of those who suffer around me. There is so much hardship on this beloved Galician soil! Whole books could be written on the misfortunes that plague working people in the fields and on the seas. I see and feel their sorrows as if they were mine. What moves me most, and which I echo in my poetry, are the endless worries of Galician women, who are loving with their own and with strangers, full of affect, hard-working in body yet gentle of heart. At the same time, their lives are so bleak that it is as if they'd been born just born to show how much exhaustion could afflict their gender. In the fields, they labour alongside men, then at home bravely bear the worries of motherhood, householding, and poverty. Often alone, they work from sunrise to sunset without help to stay alive, feed their children and care for the old. They seem condemned to find rest only in the tomb. *As my translator's mother used to say, with her Ukrainian version of retranca: "Sleep? I can sleep when I'm dead!"*

---

[3] The real vulgarity is that of self-appointed gatekeepers who admit women's words to (their) discourse only under the rubric of "diversity." Diversity from what? asks my translator. And who is in charge of "diversity"? Not the diverse, oh no... the same the same the same!

Emigration and military service take their lovers, brothers and husbands far away, depriving families of sustenance. Thus abandoned, women spend harsh lives in uncertain hope, dark loneliness, and the anxiety of unrelenting poverty. The worst is that when their men go—some drafted and others following example, need, and greed as they flee the hearth where they are loved—they leave spouses already mothers and children too young to realize, unlucky ones, that they're orphaned.

When women dare tell their secrets, weep for those alive, or yearn in sorrow, we discover such delicacy of feeling, such tenderness (even hardship can't erode it), and abnegation so huge that we look up to these brave heroines, miracles of love and endless forgiveness, whose works go unnoticed. Their stories, worthy of celestial harmonies, I can only express in the chord of the sublime, and in the key of grief. When I play that chord and key, above all in the poems of *Twice Widowed (Living and Dead)*, I know I fall short. If only I could sing all the truth and poetry of their epic, simple as it is painful.

Some have claimed that I express myself in Galician because it's good for speaking humble things. That's not the case. Most rural folk, who are Galician speakers (*but with little access to books*), are unlikely to read these verses. Yet I want to raise the problems of Galicia in our language, to repay in some way the appreciation and love that *Galician Songs*, my first book of poems in Galician, received from readers. Though a book written in the soft dialect of our country was then something new, readers embraced it, and no obstacle could stop it. I can't desert the very flag I had raised.

So here is *In Leaf. My translator offers you these poems in English, you readers and friends, not wanting praise but simple sharing, she says, of a poet whose destiny is always with the "people to come."*

Here's my wish: let the poems stream past you like a creek in summertime. Its refreshing current bears a murmur from vast solitudes, green pastures, and stunning beaches bordering the Atlantic sea. Its waters are fragrant with the countryside through which it flows, to seek its place in the hearts of all those who suffer society's indignities, *across space and time.*

May you, upon reading this book, close its covers and feel not just the ache of human living but love in your hearts for Galicia, *and for any homeland which struggling people have had to leave.*

Rosalía de Castro
Santiago de Compostela
30 March 1880

R osalía de Castro's words of formal exculpation (earnest and tongue-in-cheek at the same time) for her thinking were preceded, in the 1880 edition, by a prologue in Castilian, the language of the centre and the elites that we call *Spanish*.

It acted to shield her book from criticism of its use of Galician, shield its author from disapproval and censorship by Capital and from accusations of daring as a woman to write poetry. It is a prolix prologue by Emilio Castelar, a then well-known politician, literary journalist, historian, and friend from southern Spain who had never been to Galicia.

He parades clichés of Galician as soft and primitive, of Galicia as green and misty, and of Rosalía de Castro as merely sad. No one questions his contradictions; he is there in response to a hierarchy that disparages Galicia, to fence it off. Though his introduction is a tear or wound in the book—for de Castro now stands on her own—it is also a constituting wound.

Rosalía's anger and denunciations in her poems are never mentioned (perhaps they are the "epic poems" he doesn't like as much as he does her "intimate lyrics"), nor is any detail of what he dismisses as the "provincial grievances" of Galicia.
Two of the volumes I own of *Follas Novas* (Sálvora, 1984 and Galaxia, 1993) both banish this Prologue.

Anxo Angueira's *Follas Novas* (Xerais, 2016), a definitive scholarly text, keeps it. I decided to replace it on the next page with words from Gilles Deleuze, in homage to Rosalía de Castro, woman of the future, and to María do Cebreiro, in particular, as she has done so much to bring us better understandings of de Castro and her tremendous work in both Galician and Castilian.

Erín Moure
Montreal
2019

A PEOPLE WHO ARE MISSING –
GILLES DELEUZE

*A*rt… must take part in this task: not that of addressing a people which is presupposed already there, but of contributing to the invention of a people. The moment the colonizer proclaims 'There have never been people here', the missing people are a becoming, they invent themselves, in shanty towns and camps, or in ghettos, in new conditions of struggle to which a necessarily political art must contribute. (…)

The author finds herself before a people which, from the point of view of culture, is doubly colonized: colonized by stories come from elsewhere, but also by their own myths become impersonal entities at the service of the colonizer. The author must not, then, make herself into the ethnologist of her people, nor invent a fiction which would be one more private story: every personal fiction, like every impersonal myth, is on the side of the 'masters'. (…)

There remains the possibility of the author providing herself with 'intercessors', that is, taking real and not fictional characters, but putting these characters in the condition of 'making up fiction', 'making legends,' of 'story-telling'. The author takes a step towards her characters, but the characters take a step towards the author: double becoming. Storytelling is not an impersonal myth, but neither is it a personal fiction: it is a word in act, a speech-act through which the character continually crosses the boundary which would separate his private business from politics, and which itself produces collective utterances.[4]

Gilles Deleuze, *Cinema 2. The Time-Image*. U Minnesota Press, 1989. Transl. Hugh Tomlinson and Robert Galeta, 215-17, 220-21
http://www.lepeuplequimanque.org/en/le-peuple-qui-manque-gilles-deleuze.html

I
Vagaries
in New Leaf

II
Inner Life!
in New Leaf

III
Variations
In New Leaf

IV
Earthbound
in New Leaf

Leafless

Twice Widowed
Living and Dead

(to end every paragraph with a comma)

How to confront the challenges of the translation of Rosalía's *New Leaves*? I can't do it the way I did her *Galician Songs*. These poems are more personal, have less to prove, don't bear the nation in the same way. Personalist and intimist they are—or feign to be—and this intimacy must be marked in them somehow, for it balances and permits a civic rage, a lance of light into the civis.

Too, I want to reflect the variable orthography of the Galician, for the 19th century language was then not normativized, and yet is still readable, even for me, now, I read these *vast vagaries of the world*. To me her now "deviant" spellings as emotional markings, not blemishes but lines that mark expressions, not blemishes but flashes of the eyes regarding,

A kind of waves or wave or movement in the trees or sea,

(a way of interfering in history)*

with readings of Paul Celan's *Meridian*
and of Julia Kristeva's *Powers of Horror*

I

Of women who write of doves and flowers,
it's said they've women's souls.
And me who doesn't write of them, oh Virgin of
Paloma,[5]
        ¡argh! ¿what soul have I?

II

I know well there's naught
that's new beneath the stars;
that men have thought already
things I think up now.

    So then, ¿why do I write?
So then, because that's what we are,
clocks that tick tick tick
perpetually going round.

        (tick,

---

[5] All the frivolity that Rosalía de Castro promised in her introduction? In the first poem, we find out that she never intended it! Invoking the colonial centre of Spain, Madrid—where the Virgin of Paloma is revered and celebrated—Rosalía advises that she fully intends to be unruly, and to think.

III

      Just like clouds
     that wind impels,
and now they darken, now they harken
the mighty spaiçes of the skies,
     so the wild
     ideas that I have,
images in many forms,
of strange making, of uncertain colours,
     now obscure,
     now clarify,
the immeasurable depth of my thinking.

the tectonics of that which configures—not simply *as such*
but in a *suchness*—is here semantic, resides beyond *write* as
the poem writes *through** and its direction variegates a
meaning

*throat openi n g

IV

You'll say of these lines, and why not,
they've strange unsettled harmonies,
that in them ideas glow pale,
          like wandering embers
          which explose at times,
          which extinguish quickley,
that they ressemble the puff of soot
that wind whirls in the back garden,
and the monotone moan of pines
          on craggy shores.

I'll tell you that this is just how
my songs fly from my soul, in mayhem,
just as from deep oakwoods at first glint
          of day, emerges
          a buzz that no one can say
          if it's babble of breezes,
          if it's kiss of flowers,
these tangled, mysteryous harmonies
          that in this sad world
seek paths up to heaven , (lost)

V

In Leaf ! It makes me laugh,
this name you carry,
as if a shadow
heard folk call it light.

———

Not *In Leaf* at all; a fist
of gorse and thorns I offer:
nettles, like my sorrows;
weedy, like my grief.

———

Without scent or freshness,
savage regrets and wounds…
If in abandoned lots* you blossom,
who can blame you!!

*behind the factory for fashion fabrics
in the field where the rails were pulled up and gone, Elisa Sampedrín
wrote O Resplandor. Now a champ de possibles abides there…

18

VI

What's this buzz around me?
What's going on that I can't pin down?
I'm scared of what's
alive yet can't be seen.
I fear it's traitorous woe
that's coming; where it lands, no one can know.

VII

Some say: ¡My land!
Say others: ¡My darling!
And this: ¡My memories!
And that: ¡My friends!
All sigh, all,
for some lost treasüre.
Only I don't say a word,
only I never heave a sigh,
for my earthly body
and weary spirit
wherever I wish to go,
            go with me.

VIII

At night's apèx, there
in the light of the sad and waning lamp
or in black dreaded darkness,
            the old man sees phantoms.

―――

Some are trees withered and leafless;
            others, springs gone dry;
mountains eternally wrapt in snow;
            barrens that do not end.

―――

            And at dayb-reak,
when with the last star phantoms dissolve,
others come, sadder and more rancorous,
            for the bitter truth
they carry is scribbled in their dead eyes
            and on their hairless crowns.

―――

Never say, dear youth, you've lost the
            lilt of hope;
it's always a friend as life begïns,
and a mortal enemy only at the end!

"but in the polyvalence of the poem," adds Paul Celan in his *Meridian*,
the "I-You" has "no fixed relation"

IX

Peace, peace so craved;
for me, where is it??
Përhaps I'm not meant to…
Never had peaçe yet!!

Calm, rest,
where on earth are they?
In the aches that slay me,
in the grief they gïve me.

Peac, peace, you're a lie!
For me there's no peac e !

nail
gold
maker
pluck
yearn
clay

X

        I once had a nail
         nailed in my heart,
and I can't say now if that nail was
          gold, iron, or love.
I onely know that it pained me so deeply,
          tormented me so much
that day and night I wept as constantely
as Magda at the Cross.
         —Lord, gïven you can do all,
          I asked the Maker once,
 —gïve me the pluck to pull the nail
          out from where it lies.
         And Gdd gave it me, and I pulled it free;
         but... who'd have guessed? Now
         I felt no more torment
          nor did I know what paín was:
I only knew I didn't know what I was missing
         in the place where the nail'd been,
and prehaps, prehaps I did yearn
         for that ache…. ¡Good G/d!
This mortal clay that swaths the spírit
         who can understand it, ¡Crrisse!

Dear cadence, can an indent be an emotional marking?

To use a set of plural names open to other gods and other senses of cosmic force (a small move toward grasses that whisper light)

Rosalía de Castro was taken up by a whole 20th century of critics as a poet of nostalgia, a figure through which Galicia itself was overwritten as melancholy and yearning. 21st century cultural critics in Galicia now argue that Galicia as sentimental and melancholy is a construct, built by central Spain so as to weaken Galician national feeling (painting it as negative affect) and diminish Galician difference.

Rosalía de Castro is so much more than 'melancholy'! Her arguments are material, focus on rights and justice, and don't shrink from portraying women's lives as oppressed by poverty, economic precarity, the clergy, marriage. To call her 'melan-choly' is to vastly diminish her voice. She lays claim to no less than a (anachronic) Rancièrian "mutation in the regime of the sensible" to disorder existing poetic forms and alter what can be said using those forms, AND—particularly—what can be said by a WOMAN in using those forms.

She speaks of depression and mental illness too: ahead of her time in this, and it brings her closer to us in time. She is a clinician of the material conditions of mental and emotional life, a materialist poet. But not, no, never only, never just SAD.

To write poetry is itself a mark of agency!

(the book's most renowned poem appears in large type and out of sequence)

Cando penso que te fuches,
negra sombra que me asombras,
ó pé dos meus cabezales
tornas facéndome mofa.

Cando maxino que es ida,
no mesmo sol te me amostras,
i eres a estrela que brila,
i eres o vento que zoa.

Si cantan, es ti que cantas,
si choran, es ti que choras,
i es o marmurio do río
i es a noite i es a aurora.

En todo estás e ti es todo,
pra min i en min mesma moras,
nin me abandonarás nunca,
sombra que sempre me asombras.*+*

+"When I think you're gone, black cloud*/ that clouds me, at the ends
of my/ tresses you come back to mock me.// When I imagine you've left,
even in the sun/ you show up, and you're the star that shines, and /
are the wind that moans.//If there's song, it's you who sings, if tears, it's you/
who crys them, and you are the river murmur and are the/ night and are
the dawn.// In all you are and you are all, for me and even in me/you
abide, nor will you ever let me go,/cloud that always clouds me.

*sha dow

(a variation sung by Luz Casal)

nin me deixarás ti nunca

(a huge cloud out of place, dear reader, and *sans traduction*)

(the Human song)

there are documented effects of **chant** on **human**
physiology

no hollow is there in the wounded chest,

"and the sky wore a cravat"

"There is no chant
except the human song."
Barbu Fundoianu

a QR code and live link for reception, smartphone-accessible (as such
part thus of the hand's own gleam), prosthetic ear/eye division, absolute
as a t-shirt, gar-ment *prosthèse*, chant-based thus in polyphony,

"no hollow is there,"

"bursts"

https://www.youtube.com/watch?v=LJNMCqN7yro *Luz Casal alone...*

Nelson Eddy

Luz Casal and Carlos Nuñez

XI

When one's very joyful, very joyful,
            it seems weirdly arcane,
almost as if, it's a lie but isn't:
            joy weighs on us.

    ¡As if deep in its womb
            barren desert lies!,
that never fills with laughter or contentments,
only with harvests of bitter paiin!

            Yet when one feels regrets
            and is truly unjoyed,
there's no barrens in the wounded breast,
            grief so brims it!

So bountiful are the gifts of tribulation,
that they pour out, thank the Maker!, till her apron overflows.
            Till she who receives them,
            ¡argh! bursts with surfeit.

            In the laws of affective physics—we're stopped at times from truly
            feeling joy, yet no such stoppage halts sorrow…

XII

Today or tomorrow, who knows when?
        but mayb all too soon,
they'll come to wake me, and rather than one living,
        they'll find one dead.

———

All round me, grievous sobs
        will rise,
cries of anguish, tearbursts of my children,
        of my precious orphan babes.

———

And I without heat, unmoving, cold,
        mute, unresponsive to it all,
that's how I'll be when death leaves me
        chilled by its breáth.

———

And farewell forever, to all that I so loved!
        What dire abandon!
        Despite all the sarcasms
        that exist, must be, and ever were,
I never saw one to hush the living more
than the humble quietúde of a body deád.

To consider—in the 19th century—death as a joke on the living is to remove all
religious awe from it. Rosalía here gives us a secular poem, oh blasphemy!

XIII

    With no rancour or disdain,
nor with fear of change;
only thirst…, a thirst
for something I can't pin down; it slays me.
Rivers of life, where are you?
Air! I've got no air.

    —What d'you see in that deep dark?
What sight makes you tremble and go still?
—I don't see! I gaze as
do the blind in stárk sunlight.
And there I'll fall, there where
what falls never rises. Aagáin-

                      aerror in the pucntuation, ripple in the text
         revealing the muscle of its sonority and jump.s in sysntax

                                morning
                     self-pollinating flower
                       "excitable tissue"
      passing objects where memory loss is pleasure/
                               abyss

XIV

That hum of song and laughter,
go, come, jostle loud;
that talk of what's gone past
and what is yet to be;
that impish vitality in short,
of young folk, hits me
hard, and I tell them:
Get going, don't return.

———

One by one they paraded off
going quietly on their way,
just as beads off a rosary
fall scattered on the ground.
And the patter of their steps, in leaving,
resounds inside me,
just as, no more sadly,
in the depth of sepulchres
there might resound
the last farewell the living bid the dead.

———

At last I am alone, but so alone
that today the restless buzz of flies,
the rasping constnat gnaw of mouse,
and from the fire the snap
as from green wood
fresh sap's devoured,
all seems to speak to me, and I understand them,
they keep me company,
and my heart says trembling,
for Gawd's sake, don't go!

———

How sweet too, but sorrowfully so,
is solitude!

XV

For each beat, another:
for one pain, another pained;
upon forgetting, another forgotten,
after love, love again.

And at the end of such fatigue
and of such varied luck,
old age that grabs us by surprise
or the repose of death.

XVI

for you

When it was winter
I thought of where you'd be,
when it was sunny
I thought of where you'd head.
Now… I think only,
my love, what if you forget ! *(me)*

XVII

But see that my heart
is a centifolia rose,
and each petal is a sorrow
joined in life to another.

Pull one out, pull out two;
sorrows still I'll have to spare:
today ten, tomorr' forty,
as you pull that flower bare.

My heart you'll pull out then,
when no petals are there!

XVIII

With its deaföning and constant mormur
it lures me, the surf of this wild sea,
just as the sirens lure when singing.
—In this bed of mine mysterious and cold
the sea tells me: come softly and rest.

In love it is with me… the devil!
                and I in love with it.
We'll stay locked in stubborn battle,
for as much as surf ceàselessly calls me, I'm
death-ly afraid to go lie there.

XIX

I go in search of honey and freshness
              to wet my dry lips,
and don't know how I find, nor where,
              burning and bitters.

I go in search of nectars to sweeten
              these biting stanzas of mine,
and don't know how, nor where, always
              ferocity finds them.

              As heaven and Creátor know,
              it's not my doing;
              argh! without wanting it, I've
a hurt ailing heart.

*Et que reste-t-il d'autre, pour résister, que la dette que toute âme a contractée
avec l'indétermination misérable et admirable d'où elle est née et ne cesse de
              naître ? c'est-à-dire avec l'autre inhumain ?
De cette dette envers l'enfance, on ne s'aquitte pas. Mais il suffit de ne pas
l'oublier pour résister et, peut-être, pour n'être pas injuste. C'est la tâche de
l'écriture, pensée, littérature, arts, de s'aventurer à en porter témoinage.*
Jean-François Lyotard, *L'Inhumain*, 15

XX
¡SILENCE!

Hand nervous and heart racing,
mists condensing in my eyes,
with a world of doubt in my senses
and a world of torment in my gut,
            feeling them struggle
            in unequalled battle,
immortal desires that torment
            and rancours that kill.
I soak the sharp quill in my own blood,
            bursting the swollen vein,
and I write…., I write…. ¿Why? Go back
            to the dark pit of my soul,
            stórmy images!
Go abide with dead re-memories!
May the hand trembling over the page write only
words, and *words*, and *words*.
From the idea into form immaculate and pure
            ¿where it's still veiled?

The desire to "not write,"
"You have to make up your mind and jump,"
"Do not read this fragment…
"There is no word, pronounced…
"The poem, place where metaphor is absurd…
"Light of utopia"
And Hamlet speaks "*words, words, words*" (Act 2, Scene 2)…

(translation as a way of interfering in history)

A kind of wave or movement in the pines or sea

And a consistency as Rosalía is consistent,

so that her Galician language is somehow still readable, even though
the words are English. To create a Galician readability of surface,
where spellings are emotional markings, vowels, particularly vowels,
regarding,

With nothing to prove, but attention felt "as bliss—in the fáce of
darkness"

(to end on a comma, *détournement* or: what if the poem is vigil, holds
her keys)

"abase is not our way, R., but to speak out is to adore"

And so ends the book of thought's logicks,
embodied *ainsi*.

J-F Lyotard : *Comme toute présentation consiste dans le « mise en forme » de
la matière des données, le désastre subi par l'imagination peut s'entendre
comme le signe que les formes ne sont pas pertinentes pour le sentiment
sublime. Mais, dès lors, qu'en est-il de la matière, si les formes ne sont plus là
pour la rendre présentable ? Qu'en est-il de la présence ? 148*

I
Vagaries
in New Leaf

II
Inner Life!
in New Leaf

III
Variations
in New Leaf

IV
Earthbound
in New Leaf

Leafless
Twice Widowed
Living and Dead

FAREWELL![6]

Farewell, hills and meadows, chapels and bells;
farewell, Sar and Sarela rivers, rife with brambles;
Farewell, glad Vidán, mills and gorges;
Conxo, of sombre cloister and placid fallow;
San Lourenzo hiding, like a kid in bushes;
Balvis, place of my fondest memories;
Santo Domingos where I went in need of rest;
lives of my life, part of my very core.
And you, too, shadowed lonely walls
who've seen me weep alone and broken;
farewell, dear shadows! Farewell, detested shades!
            Once again, fortune's changes
                    drag me far away.

            ———

On my return, if I come back, all'll still be there;
the same dark hills and the same dawns
that gaze back from the rivers Sar and Sarela;
the same green fields, the same dark steeples
of the stern cathredal eyeing the horizons.
But those whom I leave now as gentle springs
or in the green of life, without tempests or tears,
when I be back, how far will they, propelled by change,
have tread along misfortune's way?
As for me..., there's nothing in the world I dread
                    but the long wait for death!

---

[6]Here the poet names rivers and neighbourhoods in the bustling capital of
Santiago de Compostela, which she left in 1879 to move with her family to
Lestrove, nearby. This first poem of the second book reverses what we
commonly consider to be "inner life," underscoring the importance of the
local, of place and surroundings, to a sense of self. *Cathredal* is her spelling
and reflects popular speech. I keep it here: the Cathredal as *catheatral*,
catharsis via theatre.

Field crickets, mole-crickets, just-born cicadas,
Toads and insects of every hue,
while in the distance, cart axles singing,[7]
such serenades of love
they always gïive us from the fields!

———

Just in remembering them,
I don't know what it does to me,
don't know if it's good
don't know if it's bad.

1.35 / 4.15 *Whiplahshh*
she's not ~~there~~ (The Zombies 1964)

---

[7]Cart axles and wheels are wood, so each cart sings when moving, wood on
wood, and each cart (made from one tree) has its own particular song. But
she's not there: the sound comes from inside her: *inner life!*

How the clouds in open spaces
    flit and wánder!
    Som-e are white,
    others dark grey;
Some seem to me as doves puffed round,
    others dispatch
    leggy light....

Divergent winds blow in the heights,
    twirl in all directions,
they púsh the clouds without order or rudder,
    don't ask me where
    and I know not why.

They lift clouds away, just as the years lift off
    our dreams,
    and our very hope.

I was there, and in that year I felt old for the first time.

Rich or poor, back then
all tarried in content and calm!
Now poor or rich, gone to the dêvil,
　　　everything, ¡all's lost!

　　　　　———

Days pass unbidden, years slip by,
　　　and even centuries will fly.
Though abundant springs go dry,
there's others yet that flow forever;
but the springs perennial in this life
　　　are always toxic.

　　　　　———

In them, the spirit that pines in hurt
bathes in the sickly damp of rancour,
　　　unable to
sip oblivion from waters meant to cure.

　　　　　———

Hate's a hellish progeny;
yet love can put an end to it. But memorie,
you! you keep recalling every slight.
　　　Yes, you!

　　　　　You're cause of ill!

V IN THE CATHREDAL

Every day, in every recess
        of the vaste temple,
old folks, nodding off,
mutter Aves and Pater Nosters;
and the archbishops in their tombs,
kings and queens, incredibly calm
in the peace of marble, sleep in tranquillity
while clerics sing in the choir.
The organ swells in sad clamours,
those of the bells, far off, answer,
and the holy image of the Redeemer
appears to sweat blood in the grotto.

Holiest Lord, at your feet,
I too sweat beads of anguish!
Though sin you always punish,
give help to the afflicted one
        who asks.

Sunset, through the stained glass image
of our Lady of Solitude, emanates serene
rays, that dress angels and the Everlasting Fatér
in hues of glory.
Saints and apostles—look! their lips
seem to move, to speak quietly
to each other, and up in the heights
of heaven, the music is about to start
as those in the greát orchestra
tune their joyful instruments.

Will they spring to life? Will they stay stone,
those countenances so realistic,
those marvellous tunics,
those eyes full of life?
You who made them with the help of the Maker,
you with the immortal name of Mestre Mateo,
from there where you humbly pose

kneeling, please answer me.
But you, with your head of curls,
santo dos croques, go silent… so I pray.[8]

   Here Glory reigns, but there,
in that bláckened arcade lies hell
and the sad souls of the damned,
there where every demon gnaws them.
I can't stop staring,
half astonished, half in fear,
for all of them do seem to me
a delirium of mortal spectres.

   How they gaze at me, those corpses
         and those demons!
How they fix on me, mocking
from the columns where they were set!
Lies, truth, which are they!
         Saints of heaven,
will they recognize me as someone
         they've seen before?
So órphaned, so grieving,
but as numb as they are…
How they afix on me…! I'm going, yes, going,
         I'm so afraid!

   But alreády in the prisms of the chandelier
         falls the final
quiet ray that afternoon sun
         serenely lays down:
and in each pretty pendant of the candelabra
         lively reflections,
scintillating like stars,
paint a thousand hues upon the floor,
and make the ghostly dust specks
seem miracles, appear portents.

---

[8]The face of the *santo dos croques* is said to be that of Mestre Mateo,
architect of the cathedral. Visitors bump heads on it upon entering,
so as to transfer wisdom from the master's stone head to their own.

But then come shadows suddenly…
All darkens, inscrutable…
Farewell, dark pearls and marvels….
Behind Mount Pedroso, Phoebus sets.

While the phantoms wander in the naves,
whispering *aves* and *pater nosters*,
old folks ask their Maker for
help that only God can give.
For when the world's about to see us off, it's then
we anxiously seek heaven.

At the feet of Our Lady of Solitude—
we've kept company for many years—
I prayed the prayer I've always prayed,
calling to mind my secrets;
for my mother I leave caresses,
for my children kisses, thousands;
it's for the tormenters of my spirit
I pray… and flee, I feel such fear.

Cathredal as catheatral:
its stones and figures and shadows speak!
In the poem, read slowly, we walk through the nave with her (the church is
unchanged today & still feels exactly like this…)

Race on, serene and crystal waves,
head out majestically in calm, as do
the shades of glorious deeds!
Roll past, relentless, just as
countless generations roll to eternity
in contemplating you just as I do…
Give me your perfume, pretty roses;
to my thirst that burns, may clear sprins
quench its fire; clouds of mist,
protect me with your veil of delicate lace
from glaring rays of ardent sun;
and you, soft touch of breeze,
strike up mysterious concerts
amidst the oaks at the dark rim of pastures
past which the Sar flows, murmuring softly.

Time flees quickly; perhaps even lightning
falls more slowly across the immensity of space
than do the years passing.
For me, they race past in fierce battle…
and have raced by me just the same… ¡and day arrives…!
Give me your kísses and embrace me
here by the river, in meadow-fresh grasses…
Don't tell anyone where I am, amid flowers
which I wish would hide
my telltale wound….; may my body never be dislodged
by profane hands that lift me elsewhere…
I want to stay here where my grief abides!

To live in summer heat beside a river, yes this is inner life….

Every night I pondered tearful...
hoping vast night would not stay,
and yet it lasts... and lasts... amidst it
                    may the night of sorrow
                    enfold my keening...

But the insolent light of day,
                    steady in its betrayal,
                    each and every dawn
penetrates radiant with glory
right to the bed where I lay stricken
                    with my afflictions.

Ever since, I seek night
                    deep and dark,
and I crave darkness in vain, for always
night's sweep ends with dawn...
Only inside me, seeking darkness
                    and entering shadow,
a night has arrived that is unending:
                    in my stricken soul.

2am, *the suicide hour.* "simply being awake at night may be a risk factor"
https://www.sciencedaily.com/releases/2014/06/140602102004.htm

echoing Novalis, says Angueira

I fell so low, so low,
light cannot reach me;
I've lost sight of stars
and abide in darkness.

But wait…! Why do you laugh,
insensitive to struggle!
I'm still alive…, I can still
rise to take revenge.

Casting stones at those downfallen,
go ahead and cast a hundred,
cast, and when you stumble,
you'll all get yours.

from I *singular,*
to you *singular,*
to you *plural,*
the stanzas open and trace their path: an amplification.

May this cup from which you drink
                    life's sweetness,
bear a drop of gall, just one,
squeezed from my pining heart.
                    You'll undertand then
how paine softens cold stones,
                    though it can't soften
ironclad souls and vicious hearts.

she addresses the reader.   it's as if we see that drop of gall coming, and jump aside, and it lands at our feet, dissolving stone.

x SWEET LOVES

Like the scent of roses that rises from the branches
on a morning in May, there are sweet loves
felt on arrival, though they enter unseen
through the cherished door that the heart opens them
willingly, just as in August
the flower opens in afternoon mist.

And without murmur or complaint, or tears, or tune,
soft and wistful, like the breath of angels,
they incarnate purely in us, move in our blood
and turn the barrens green in spirit wherever they abide.
Seek these loves, seek them
if you have one who can give you this love,
for these loves are all that's lasting
in this fleeting life.

xi MEAN LOVES

It was ache and cholera,
was fear and aversion,
was a love lopsided,
castigation from Above!
There are mean loves, that weigh heavily,
that deprive spirits, that cloud consciences,
that bite when they caress, that burn with their gaze,
that give angry pain, that stain and confront.
Better to die of cóld
than warm yourself at their hearth.

> Open wide, new roses:
>   gleam, carnations:
> in their garden, trees are vested
>   in pretty leaves of green.
> Vines that once lent us shade,
> you return to cover us with amazements.
>   Beautiful nature,
>   eternally the same,
> tell all mortals, tell again those driven mad
>   they too w'll perish no more!

XIII FREE OF CHARGE...

> When they tuck the shroud around me
>   if I bear one;
> when they lay me in the coffin
>   if I get one;
> when they intone the responses
> —if there's wherewithal to pay the clergy—
> and when down in the grave....
> even if Saint Peter does raise me,
> if only I don't bust a gut laughing
> just at the thought of it!
> ¡What a burial! For they have to bury me
> even if no one pays them...

Light and progress everywhere…, but
            doubts still linger,
and tears come for no reason,
and griefs seem to have no why.

———

Same old tune, they say, tired
of this chorus, they who keep arriving, and leave
in fresh batches, to wander blindly
            seeking what doesn't exist.

———

—¡Reprobates!… Always probing in the dark
            which mutely tells you nothing.
Seek the faith you lost in doubt,
            and quit your sighing.

———

But they, too, lost,
head up one path and down another,
with no idea, suckers! where they go,
            without peace, direction, without faith.

. . . .

Sad's the song we're singing.
But what if there's no better song?
            Greát light blinds the eyes,
and greát desire makes us anxious.
            When plagues befall us
            one after another, we can't do more
            than hurriedly bury our dead,
            duck our heads, and hope
the waves of sickness pass us by…
            ¡Pass by!… for others will come.

It is so beautiful where I was ~~today~~ lonely

They howled at me as I walked on,
                nearly exhausted,
without energy but deep in thought
and with the fatal poison I carried.
                And those whose paths I crossed,
                on seeing me struggle,
in my pain and my affront,
                the turncoats mocked me
(and did so as soon as they guessed).
                —If they knew my pain, dear Gdd,
I thought, trembling, even the current
                of the river would turn against me.

                ⸻

Seeking shelter by the highest walls,
                on deserted roadways,
bloodying my feet on sharp gravel,
I was nearly at the place I loved,
imagining with excitement: —Will my babes
                still be awake?
Oh, if they see me arrive so battered,
tearful, breathless and bleeding,
they'll be so shaken, my poor babies,
                at seeing their unlucky mother!

                ⸻

Little by little I went on,
and climbed the stairs in fear,
my sad heart leaping:
¡I listened! Not even the buzz of flies.
In the cradle my angels still slept,
                protected by the Virgin Mother.

the destitution of rape or forced prostitution echoes here, alongside
the mother-love that surpasses all destitution...

Why, sweet soul of mine,
why do you not crave now
¿what you once craved?

———

Why, thoughts,
why do you not thrive now
¿upon desires you hold dear?

———

Why, my spirit,
why do you now feel humiliated,
¿when once you were proud?

———

¿Why, heart,
why do you not speak now
sweet words of love?

———

¿Why do you no longer throb
with the soft pulse
that calms all worry?

———

¿Why, finally, my Maker,
am I bereft so long of both
earth and heaven?

———

And you, rósy star
that it's said was born
to guide me, you'll be able

—

go dim forever,
having been unable to
forever light my way!

A poem that can never be simply "sad"; it warns of a mighty struggle
for mental health. Rosaliá here pens—intently—the words of one about
to take their own life.

Her last 4 lines are built on *able* and *forever*,
then both words are reversed, like a twist of knife or the
contradictions in, say, a sleeping pill that instead of sleep, gives
suicidal ideations...

Cathredal bell
grave, sad, and sonorous,
when, at the glimmer of day
you peal the peal of dawn
in silent space,
resounding melancholy;
your striking chimes
awaken feelings I scarce recall.

———

Some were pure
as the glow of dawn,
others like the hope
which lovers dream,
and the last were restless,
half light, half shadow,
haff a nameless pleasure,
and half a dread surprise.

———

¡Oh! how years have run by
and dawns passed,
and luck worn thin,
and worries grown.
Now when you resound, bell,
when you strike the stroke of dawn,
My eyes brim and I break
into quiet tears.

———

How müted and sadlye,
how fearfully you echo
in my waiting ear,
messenger of the dawn
which at daybreak
you solemnly toll....!
Where did my wakenings
to fortune and glory go?

—

They're gone forever;
but you, grave and sonorous,
oh, at the break of day,
with your melancholy voice
you daily see and show us
every nascent dawn;
and it seems that their death,
and mine, is what you toll.

—

Cathredal bell,
so grave and so sonorous,
¿why do you keep sounding
each clear dawn
so that I must hear you
and dissolve in tears?
But so soon,..., so soon, my ears
will not hear you, in evening or at dawn.

the sound of churchbells draws
even those outside religion
and this draw
draws Rosalia to write this secular prayer

Sea with your fathomless waters;
sky with your immensity;
help me bury the phantom
that terrorizes me.

It's bigger than your every force,
and further it extends…
with one foot where the stars gleam,
and the other where they dig my grave.

Implacable cruel trickster,
always just ahead of me,
it threatens to pursue me
even to eternity.

pursued by a circle of fire ahead, the paradox of
the mind's doubts—
which enable thought
but ache the spirit…

Dig quickly, dig down,
gigantesque thought,
dig a deep pit where all memory
of the past we'll both inter.
¡Let the dead slip under!
¡Dig, dig quickly!

And give it for a stone the dark surround,
and give it the void for a cemetery ground.

In thinking that you've gone,
black cloud that clouds me,
at the ends of my tresses,
you come back to mock me.
        In imagining that you've left,
you show up in the sun itself,
and you're the star that shines,
and are the wind that moans.
    If there's song, it's you who sings,
if tears, it's you who crys them,
and you are the river murmur
and are the night, and are the dawn.
    You are in all and you are all,
for me and even in me you abide,
nor will you ever let me go,
cloud that always clouds me.

oh poem, we already know you!

In Galician, verbs do not need *I*...
so I translate "When I think" as "In thinking" and "When I imagine"
as "In imagining" to background the constituted I in English too.

A poem of deepest inner life, here the reflexive self—the I—cannot be
touched, but is at the same time *so profoundly touched* it cannot even
arise: the paradox of depressive illness but also of a nation
unacknowledged and denied autonomy.

For Galicians, this poem is an anthem. Sung by the greatest voices, and
once heard, you hear it forever. The poem—as Angueira and do
Cebreiro insist—is radical in its contemporaneity of structure and
evocation.

¡Arise, missing peoples!

Tremble if a stroke of greát luck
catches you on this earth by surprise;
superhuman glories, here
bring supreme mishaps.
Don't even think that hurt will pass
as whims do on this earth;
there are hells in memory,
even when the conscience is clear!

As ivy roots across high walls,
in some hearts aches take root,
and som-e of them crumble life
as ivy roots do stone.
Yes, tremble when on this earth
you feel a surge of luck:
better that your life just flow
as do serenity's pools.

Lead me to that clear fountain
        where together we sip
the purest waters that quench
desire's flame and love's thirst.
Lead me by the hand as you once did…
        But no, I fear
        I'll see in its clear liquid
        the shadow of the dark
disappointment without cure or consolation
        that time's lodged between us.

THE LOVE LETTER, READ YEARS LATER....

XXIII **AT THE MANOR OF…** *ummm?…*

        Late afternoon it was,
the trill of the crickets alreády rising;
        water roared loudly over the dam,
and fugitive fires flickered distant.
Below the mountain, the chérished manor
stood majestic in the darkening village,
        with the ancient olive
as curtain for its window.
        The staircase was deserted,
        the paternal nest stood empty,
and over it, falling mysteriously
in the dusky shadow, was oblivion.

        Who's to look to the past
        with compassionate gaze?
        Who's to recall the dead,
when even the living can't remember?

In the skies, blue so clear;
on the ground, green intensity;
in the depth of my soul,
all's sombre and dark.
   What joyful parade!
What laughter and ease!
And my eyes even so
are full of tears.
   Swathed in green,
the fields gleam afresh,
while bitter gall
dews my heart.

beauty's ache and the sublime
(longinus, burke, de castro, rilke, lyotard)

Those known as honourable in town,
stole from me my every brightness,
cast muck on my finery in a single day,
and threw me an old smock in tatters.
   They left not a stone where I'd lived;
homeless, without abode, I lived in the potato heap;
slept rough in the meadows with the hares;
my children… my angels whom I so loved,
they died, died for hunger killed them!
   I was dishonoured, they tarnished my life,
left me a bed of thorn and bramble;
while they, malicious weasels,
slept calmly in a bed of roses.

———

   —¡Save me, oh judges! I yelled… Crazy hope:
the judges mocked me, and justice sold me out.
   —¡God, help me G/d! I cried, and yelled again…
but from on high, no diety heárd me.
   That's why, like any hurt or wounded she-wolf,
in a raging lunge I grabbed the sickle,
swung slowly up… Not even grass felt it!
And the light hid, and the wild beast slept
companionablly in a feather bed.

   I watched them calmly, and raised my hands,
with a single whack, I left them lifeless.
And satisfied, I sat down with the victims,
quiet, waiting for day to dawn.

   And so…, so justice prevailed:
I, over them; and the laws, over the hand that smote them.

For Rosalía, this is a poem of inner life! The revolution is intimate.
A refusal to be cast outside (Kristeva).

Grd casts a veil over
our very hearts,
veil that hides abysses
on which only s/he can gaze.
    When I think what would happen,
while I'm bowing in adoration
humble, on my knees
as one does to adore a lord,
    if this veil between heart and abyss
were suddenly to slip;
I tremble… and bowing lower
say: —my gosh, Grd is wise!

¡Swish-flick! ¡Swish-flick! In night's silence
sinister fingers move back and forth,
      while the digital numerals
that time each instant in black,
      on the implacable screen
slowly add up on its limpid face.
      All around is dark
      and only in the immense heights,
in sky's limitless depth
some restless star glows
just as, in the ash of a spring burn,
a few earthy sparks still live in cinders.
   And the fingers keep tapping
like heartbeats, filled with ache,
      amid the resonance of light
      in thick darkness.
The fearful eye gazes at this light
      in darkness;
one silent instant after another
passes, and others arrive silently
in their wake, falling into eternity
as grain does upon the stone;
so that sleep, in the bright of mortal eyes,
      can't lower its weighty mist.

Here, Rosalía's "¡Tic-toc, tic-toc!" is given an anachronic twist. Today it
is the screen-lights that prevents sleep, for clocks no longer tick. Yet
time's beat still defeats us at night: *our fingers, its pendulums...*

XVIII STONE FRIENDS

When amid the triste and chilly naves
       between high walls,
so cold they are, so sad,
when in the evening I go to pray,
what crazy and strange thoughts
flit in my head!

———

Deafening silence I know so well,
it's been my friend all these years,
full of many memories,
and while the spirit seems to hear
       its mortal echo,
in the greát basilica's spaces
silence reigns with mysterious serenity.

———

Quavering shadows, tremouring rays,
       by the altar
they settle, wander, flee, and loom
       from front to back.
And the holy Apostle, seated eternally
       on his dais
of silver and gold, stiffly contemplates
all that's there, with staring eyes.

———

If only I were saint, were stone,
       like those found here!
Like Saint Pete, holding keys,
or Johnny Baptiste, one finger held high,
I'd have seen generations pass
       one after another,
without fear of life and its torments;
without fear of death, that so shakes us.

———

Soon enough our sad pilgrimage
        draws to an end.
People pass on, like clouds
        of summer.
And stones remain… , and when I die,
        cathredal,
you, dark pile, weighty and sad,
when I'll no more be, you'll be still.

XIX

In the sway of May, long May,
    all is draped in roses;
for some, they dress the dead,
    for others, marriage poses.

In the sway of May, long May
    you held short sway óver me;
with you came my happy luck,
    with you, it turned to flee.

Moon faded
to the hue of pale gold,
you see me and I don't want you
to see me, from so high.
As you're crossing space,
lift me quietly on your rays.

———

Star to orphans,
faded moon,
I know well you won't light
sadness such as mine.
Go tell your Maker
and ask I be lifted up to where a Maker bides.

———

But you ask nothing,
faded moon,
and not in this world nor
in another, will I find fortune.
If you know where death
tends its dark abode,
then ask death to lift my body and soul together
to where no one will remember,
not in the world where I am nor in the heights, above.

How placidly they glow
river, fountain, sun!
How they shine…, but their shine is not
for me, no.

———

How they flourish, grass and bushes
how the buds flower in the trees!
But their flourishing or flowering is not
for me, no.

———

How they sing, the birds,
their amorous songs!
but though they sing, their song is not
for me, no.

———

How beautiful Nature casts
a smile at May's caress!
But the smile is not
for me, no.

———

Yes… for all there's glints of
air, light, warmth for all…
But in this all there's none
for me, no.

———

¡And so!... since in this place I find no
air, no light, no soil nor sun,
will there not be a tomb for me?
For me, no.

By the worn veranda
grizzled with ivy and lilies
she went to sit quietly and sadly
        across from the old chapel.

———

The interminable procession of the Dead,
some still embodied, some in spirit,
slowly appeared upon the crest
        of the road ahead,
glowing steady and pale,
like clothes hung across a lawn.

———

She contemplated how they passed and passed,
        filing on together to infinity,
        without gazing upón her
with their dull and sunken eyes
        that gave no sign or hint
of once having known her.

———

And some were her lovers in the past,
some were family, others friends,
        childhood playmates,
        servants and neighbours.
But passing and passing in front of her,
the dead just pressed forward
        walking indifferently
        the road of infinity,
while the silent night drew close
        its sad bereavements
around a stranger in her own land,
        who, without abode or ally,
sat on the veranda watching
how their fleeting flickers glówed.

¡Padrón…! ¡Padrón…!
Santa María… Lestrove…
       ¡Farewell! ¡Farewell!

       I

   That laughter unending,
that frolic without pain,
that crazy happiness,
       why did it end?
   Those sweet melodies,
those loving murmurs,
those serene nights,
       why are they gone?
   The sonorous quiver
of harpstrings and the sounds
of wistful guitar,
       who took them?
   Everywhere mute silence,
       loneliness, ache,
where once luck itself
       alone reigned…

   ¡Padrón…! ¡Padrón…!
Santa María… Lestrove…
       ¡Farewell! ¡Farewell!

       II

   The Adina cemetery
is enchanting, it's true,
with its dark olive trees
ever fondly recalled;
with its carpet of grasses and
flowers, pretty as any of the Maker;
with its retired clerics
sitting outside to take the sun;
with children who play there
ebullient and glád;
with pale flagstones laid down,

and with a damp heap
of earth, where some poor soul
was interred at dawn.
  Long have I loved you,
enchanting simetery,
with your dark olives
older than my grandparents;
with your venerable priests,
who go to sit in the sun
while birds raise in chorus
their matinal refrains,
and with your ossuary, humble
yet imposing respect
when the light that burns in it
shines resplendent at night.
I've loved you greátly and still do,
even the Maker knows this is true;
but today, thinking of you
my heart clouds over,
for the earth is upturned,
        dark, bereft of flower.

¡Padrón...! ¡Padrón...!
Santa María... Lestrove...
        ¡Farewell! ¡Farewell!

        III

  I went one day to seek them,
heart pounding aloud,
I went calling each one
and none gave reply.
  I knocked at one door then another,
sensed no speech or voice
and as if in an empty tomb
my knock echoed.
  I looked through the lock,
what silense...! what fear...!
saw but wandering shadows
that passed without sound,

72

like wisps that float upward
in a ray of bright sun.
    My hair stood on end
from eeriness and grief.
Not one…! not any…!
Where are they? What became of them?
    The sad sound of the bell
slowly reached me…
Death had taken them! it pealed.

    ¡Padrón…! ¡Padrón…!
Santa María… Lestrove…
        ¡Farewell! ¡Farewell!

the exiled, the expelled, the succour of death and the dance of the I…

Shine, ray of dawn,
in a dream of peace clear and bright.
To one born blind, what does
your divine blaze matter?

———

Sigh, serene waves,
as winds moan through the pines.
¡Music, oh! and songs and harmonies,
to the deaf, what good are they?

———

Keep going, pass by, you beauties,
you cure all who hope and love.
Loves and pleasures, though, are just a lie
to those who bear their souls worn dry.

Why, God of pity
why do they call it crime
to seek the death so long in coming,
when a person's life
exhausts and afflicts her?

———

Heavy with sorrows,
what heart can resist?
What tired traveller does not crave
to seek the rest
theyir body begs for?

———

Why if one can't quëll
the hurts that ôppress,
why's it said you'll be angry
if such a person bows low
into the tomb?

———

Hell on earth
or hell without end
beyond that deep pit of the grave
that the soul craves
but that eyes can't gauge.

———

If it's really true,
and as truth, it's terrible,
you either grant lonely hell
to the many who keep enduring,
or if you don't, holy Maker, oh… ¡pity on the sad!

Against the theological interdiction of suicide: again, the tension between outside and inside that makes thinking beings. (thinking Kristeva's *Power of Horror* here)

Clear were the days,
laughing the mornings,
and yet her own sadness
dark as orphanhood.
    She came at dawn's light,
returned at evening's...;
but whether she comes or goes
no one seeks to know.
    One daylight she took
the trail along the dunes...
As no one awaited,
she returned no more.
    Three days passed before
the sea released her,
and there where the crow rests
she lies, interred alone.

sadness makes orphans of us
in a world that is in fact not sad, for the natural world fills it and us,
its inhabitants

but this does not absolve her or us or many of affliction
(sh/we are of a mind)

and the sea's roar is death's orator

the theological interdiction against suicide, railed at in the second-
last poem, here is achieved, leaving the social empty, for she is
buried alone outside the community of the graveyard.
Thus ends the book of *Inner life!*

I
Vagaries
in New Leaf

II
Inner Life!
in New Leaf

III
Variations*
in New Leaf

IV
Earthbound
in New Leaf

Leafless
Twice Widowed
Living and Dead

*with an insistence on women's desire!

THERE'S NO WORSE CURSE (HEARTBREAK)

–dialogue of the mother, the daughter, and the aristocratic lover–

I

—Sweet Mariana, get thee to the river.
—I beg, my mother, that here I may stay,
that I not see the light of day,
that light itself not see me.
—What's this you're saying, lass…?
—That yesterday morning in the meadow
the wyater turned red
when I went to bathe there;
and below my foots
it was staining grasses:
that the sun in hitting my face
turned me a waxen colour;
and the shells of chestnuts
tangled in my hair;
the thorns of thornbushes
savagely bit me;
in going down the paths
brambles snagged me;
nettles stung me;
dunes startled me,
and wee birds in seeing me
intoned a mournful plaint:
¡Sweet Mariana's going to die…!
¡Everyone, pray for M!

—¡Oh, our Lady of Carme,
my daughter is ill!
¡Oh, Gdd, they've cursed her!
¡Argh, a witch blew foul on her!
If you weren't so pretty,
no one would envy you.
Gïft of my own womb,
come to me, don't worry,
go ask help of St. Peter the Martyr,
he does more than sell bulls and cows…
—Loving mother, my mother,

78

you can bring me where you wish,
but for me there's no cure
anywhere on earth,
it's just that a heart
holds me in chains,
and it's just that a foul mouth
has badly cursed me ...

—Who cursed you, my daughter?
What evil, sweet child, did you dö?
—Don't even ask, my mother,
it's best you not know.
The secrets of this curse
are best left asleep under stones.
—Speak, lass, I feel
the blood boil in my veins.
—Better had I not seen light of day
that light'd never seen me...
Loving mother, dear mother,
don't curse me as did the witch.
Let me go with my secraet
to sleep deep in the ground.
—You'll not go with your secraet;
you'll not go, though you wish;
your mother will follow you askiing
and there you'll answer.
—¡Oh, my mother! He was pretty
as angëls are in churches,
his loving murmurs
far, far smoother than silk;
he was sweet... much sweeter
than honey from the comb.
He smelled of May roses,
his eyes were stars,
and like pure gold were
his curly locks...
—Stop, Mariana, stop,
my heart is breáking...
Who is this? tell me, tell me...
Or maybe it was a dream, my lass?

—It was no dream, Mamai, I do not dream,
though I really wish I did.
I dallied with the Count, my lady,
the Countess's own betrothed.
He spoke to me in the oaks
when I was gathering firewood;
he spoke to me at the river
on serene summer eves;
I talked to him..., oh I'd talk
Mum dear, for the rest of my life!
—Oh dear blessed Virgin,
my daughter's taken ill,
ill with heartbreák
that did her very honour ill.
No wonder the birds sang to you,
dear Mariana, my treasure:
¡Sweet Mariana's going to die!
¡Pray for her, everyone!

Sweet Mariana withers,
the poor lass's gone pale,
she's touched no food,
no waater she wishes.
Friends cannot console her,
no music cheers her,
at the sight of sun she wheezes
at the sight of flowers she shakes.
Her mother's going crazy
seeking heäling herbs,
which she places nightly
on Mariana's pillow,
and she goes to every hermitage,
with offering upon offering
to every blessed Virgin,
to all the saints, she prays
and lights candles in the niches
so the dead will intercede.
But Mariana does not recover,
Mariana still lies pale...
All say that a vampire

comes in the dark to suck her blood,
some say they've seen at night
the wandering souls in the village.

II

—Your lovestruck lass is dying from what?
Because of me, this beauty's dying?
¡Never! For it's unbefitting
to my very nobility.
Dry up those tears,
stop crying, old woman,
that girl of flowing tresses
will soon be my Countess.
We'll go now to tell her,
we'll go together to her side.
    And off they set at a fine trot
through the meadow.

    —Oh Sire…, ¿don't you hear crows?
They're heading from the village…
Look at their wings beat…
just as black wings do.
—Let wings beat, crows
shów off like that when flying.
—Sire, sire…, ¡how they caw!
¡heir caw augurs something!
It's that they foretell death,
there's death here nearby.
—¡Perhaps! May God embrace
the one who takes leave of earth.
—Oh Sire, they're tolling death…
¡Oh! it's our own churchbell ringïng…
¡My Virgin! ¿Who'd be dying?
—Don't think about who'll die,
old girl, think only
of your daughter ailing.
—Sire, sire…, we've far to go;
lay on the lash, for gosh sake,

for when I left, at dawn's brink,
none lay ailing in the village
but my daughter,
who was the colour of earth,
with feet like cold snow,
and tiny hands like wax,
and all around her sad eyes
something like dark circles.
—You scare me with your words,
and impatience assails me...
I'd give half my lands
to spare her life:
the most beautiful lass
there is in all the region.
If it's that we find her dead,
if that's what we'll be finding...
If she dies, until my death
I must do penance.

　　She died, did Mariana;
the Count saw her in candlelight,
but she did not see him;
she'd died before he came.
She died just like a little bird,
and in the shroud that holds her
she's like an ángel who awaits
for heaven to come for her.

....
....

　　No one knew she'd died of love
and of being forgotten;
some said a plague
had sent her to her tomb;
others said it was a witch
who blew a foul stink on her...
But for her, the Count did
penance till his life's end.

(call and response)

The book of variations is a book in multiple voices, in poems of conversation or dialogue, and here dialogue includes silence, and listening, as dialogic forms. It also privileges women's desire. The book is a thinking that is thus an orchestration, that does not come from one viewpoint. A tradition of call-and-response is at work here, yes, but Rosalía's purpose is not simply to evoke popular forms.

The first poem reworks a conversational tale from the tradition of oral romance, "Mariana and the Count of Andrade," collected (and already manipulated in his archiving) by Manuel Murguía, Rosalía's husband, a historian, journalist, and ethnographer.

The story's appeal to the poet lies clearly in the effects on women of differences in class and standing, particularly in matters of desire. As such, it is an economic poem. As are most of the poems in the book of variations.

We can see the effect of these dialogic workings of Rosalía de Castro in Galician culture today. For example: in the poetry of Chus Pato, who also has used multiple voices and dialogues in her poems. Each is the postmodern poet of her times, and their voices both have economic import, and plead for a different economy: a *different repartition of the sensible*, to quote Jacques Rancière.....

—I've three white hens
  and one black rooster,
gonna lay us good eggs
  when the time comes;
gonna sell them high
  in January;
gonna save the moolah
  for a pretty mantilla;
gonna dress in it
  at my wedding;
gonna...

  —Hey, there, Marica
  go fetch me a pint,
and don't take off
  those rags for now,
let the hens hang out
  with the black rooster,
so they lay their eggs,
  and never mind that guff
about January, moolah
  and weddings,
love o' my life,
  it's time to get drinking!

Marica, figure of fun in popular rhyme, is recuperated here by Rosalía to create a refraction that tells of the status of women in marriage without making further comment. The status of women outside marriage is examined in the next two poems....

III

  —A true love is greát and blessed,
    delight of all delights,
and it's sweet… sweeter than all sweetness.
    —Perhaps that's why, so often
one way or another,
it causes "heartburn," as everyone knows.
    —But if it ends with a wedding?
    —Even if in a wedding it ends;
love's just like any dessert, my dear,
    as everyone knows
    like they know fire burns,
the more you eat, the more you regret it later.

IV

  —Don't sing, don't cry, don't laugh, don't talk,
don't enter, don't leave without my permission.
In the name of St. Peter, just gïve me some room!
  —Well that's how it goes, child, don't be cranky,
for if you sing, cry, laugh, and talk…
Who let the dog out? they'll soon say of you, girl.

V ¡ALERT!

In spooky darkness
and the raucous murmur of wild pines
that the storm tosses and enslaves,
there was heard, as if a fox's yelp,
a fearful whistle.

———

A dread lament to make blood run cold
answered the fearful whistel,
from deep in the thicket,
escalating the sadness the spirit feels
at the hoarse murmur of the border river.

———

Between dark banks gentle and slow,
just as resigned thoughts flow
between sad remorse and hope,
wind came like a compass needle
spinning from the furthest reaches.

———

But at the edge of the wide bank,
mysterious and crouched, a sentinel
in a Miño skiff was resting;
with gun in hand and wakeful,
through the branches he kept watch.

(...)

fragmentation and longing
in the silence of surveillance:
fleeing across Galicia's southern border into Portuguese hills...

The two-part poem that's next, and the one to the left, form a diptych. In the first poem the scene is described by a voice off-camera, and we see but the shadow of the border guard along the Miño *(the river that forms the border between Galicia and Portugal)* and of his weapon, signifying his readiness to kill whatever moves. We, who must be silent, receive his silence too.

In the second poem, the dialogue between the fleeing couple marks the first part; the second part holds the woman's frightened voice alone—the man's is silent.

The two parts are hinged together, as are the two poems.

We too are in the dark. *Is the man dead and the woman found? Is the* phantasm of her remorse *a child to come?*

In this *variation*, nature (wind, trees) speaks, people speak, the sentinel is silent. All moves except the sentinel. Migrancy, propelled by the desire to love freely, is the subject here. *Trepidation and fragility reign....*

I

—All's dark, shadows couch the pathway,
and not even heaven has eyes, nor pinewoods tongues.

———

Let's go! Who knows the depth of what's hidden?
There's no soul who knows! Come! Night's dark.

———

—Dark? but there's a glow of some treacherous light…
—It's a star that glows in roiling waters.

———

—And don't you hear something rustle in the grass?
—It's the wind gone crazy, twirling foliage.

———

—Listen, I feel footsteps, and some shape hulks there…
—If it's alive, we'll kill it; it won't talk if it's dead!

———

—But here by this headland, there's a deep hole:
come on, and we'll see if saint or devil finds us there.

II

And where'm I heading? Where'll I hide?
So that no one sees me and I see no one.

The light of day amazes me, starlight astonishes me.
And men's stares penetrate my very soul.

And it's that whatever is inside me, can be seen
on my face, just as tides deliver up their dead, at last.

It could be, and let it be seen ¡….! but no: I bear you
inside me: terrifying phantasm of my remorse!

Immense elms, myrtles
that flaunt white flowers,
some still just budding,
others wind-plucked of petals,
boxwoods already centuries old
that go green together,
their branches and trunks forming
walls no one can penetrate,
where tired serpents make
burrows in which to nest.
Bay trees, kin of boxwoods
in height and in origin,
now rooted timeless
deep in the earth.
Lemon and orange trees
that green moss shades
spread the scent of their blossoms
which reinvigorates us all.
Eternal forests in which
mysterious shadows reign,
crossed only by birds
down sad leafy lanes
where the murmur of rivulets
sounds almost a plaint,
and where summer's sun
penetrates with melancholy.
And in the midst of this thicket
and this beautiful sadness,
in a house even sadder still,
but with proud façade,
there they say is the nest
of the mother of all witches:
house with cedar doors,
grilles in each window,
kitchen vast as those of monks,
silence as in churches,
servants who never speak,

dogs that bite like beasts.
There they see her black and thin
as a starving cat,
in the most vigorous and flourishing
of our beautiful Galician earth.
And these evils that afflict us
it's said she brings them all....
For, as often happens in this life:
Those at fault won't bear the burden!

The relation of social exclusion and misogyny... The poem uses a
folkloristic structure for political ends: to decry those who use
superstitions about women to explain poverty. And who ignore the
conditions of women left alone by emigration, driven mad and silent
at home by hierarchies of the village. In this poem, as well, the natural
world speaks: *it too is an interlocutor, as important as humans.*

TO EVERYTHING ITS TIME

    From happy May, a fresh dawn
makes you smile in melancholy autumn,
and at Christmas, stiff limbed,
you gladly warm yourself in August sun:
then you shivered fearful, and went seeking
deep and restless shade;
but lazy memory, too late
        paid you mind
        that these sudden, rare
        untimely change-ups
of struggle and worry, in this life,
are always the surest signs.
And in the heat lent you in winter
        by thoughts of August sun
you felt but the mortal cold of fever
        that froze you to the bones.
        To everything its time
        And to each ferality its den.

Or Hamlet: *Act 1, scene 5*
    The time is out of joint—O cursèd spite,
that ever I was born to set it right!

Beside the flowers, the girl
happily sings her sweet song,
and she's fair as a lily,
pale as moonlight.
Aside her sweet mouth, a pretty mole
placed by the Maker, shaped so perfectly
it charms us all.

———

Tint of moonlight... ¡lovely colour!
two eyes like dark night,
lips that speak smiling,
and oh that mark... Beauty
greáter has been had by no creature,
than the beauty the Creator willed you, lovely rose,
sweet, pure, and gorgeous.

———

Being loved, that's your hallmark,
loved more than anyone ever was,
and ¡what lucky fate!
to be loved and to love well.
This is woman's very ambition
and the sole good she seeks unstinting
in this wretched life.

———

But, beauty-marked lass,
do you know the saying?
Unlucky in love is
she who bears such a mark.
And they do say you're ill-fated
despite the laugh on your lips
that know no grievance.

When we die (and I know, having been among the dying) the only accomplishment we care about is love...

———

      Sooner or later,
    in this thing of falling in love
    bad luck the traitor will
    fast be at work.
    And cast its spell on
innocent hearts and pure souls
      not meant for bitterness.

———

. . . .
. . . .

      Woe for the lass marked
    pale as moonlight!
    How she sings her song
    serene and unknowing
that she, marked by beauty, luck shall elude,
      that's how her life will go.

———

      Happy-go-lucky she sings
    some pretty chanson,
    that brings to her mind
    such cherished memories,
    that is thus like a prayer
that the soul, sad, lovingly murmurs
      asking the Lodestar for fortune.

———

      And she doesn't realize, silly,
    and doesn't imagine, poor thing,
    that evil walks in love's footsteps,
    and her luck will wither
    if she's one born touched by beauty:
she of such exquisite marking
      will never know repose.

———

Only grief awaits you,
lovely rose, marked by beauty;
greát grief following small,
one upon another will knock
at your door as they arrive;
and no one, such is destiny's power,
can turn your luck around.

x A ROLLING STONE

She started out by thinking;
after that, she liked to think;
and from liking to desire,
goes more quickly as you sink.

——

And daily wending downward,
downward without stop:
from desiring to the sinful,
you quicken as you drop.

¡ Oh, Thought !

—a conversation with the deity, the for who else to address on mental health?—

Why's it exist? Who is it? Where's its proud
home? Artful, how does it thrive?
Light sleep or passing cloud
is all it is for many, hardly leaves a trace.
Other feel its perfidious blows
lay seige to them with dark treachery
from start to end of life's toil.
But they never see it, though they look
all round to avoid it; how many are there
who never feel its pestilent breath
in air or space, nor on earth nor on the sea,
though it's everywhere, ever damaging.

. . . .

Evil is the child of hell, good that of heaven;
whose is woe? She-wolf
never sated who redoubles her furor
on sighting a deep and bloody wound.
Where's it come from? What's it want? Why'd you let it,
mighty Maker, when you see us suffer?
Can't you tell, oh Potentate, that its power suffocates
faith and love, in the spirit that had faith in you?
How it hardens a heart that once
was every softness! How it kills
light in hope, so that hope's peaceful gleam
amid the stars is struck from existence,
light that lent new strength to tired feet
and renewed courage in the timorous soul!
All rots in its passage, its damned plaint
chokes everything forever:
it sticks its muck to everything.
And what a deep pit it digs around
whomever it pursues! How folk
flee from it so as to block the laments
its pain provokes, or the frightening

blasphemy that with trembling lip
it pronounces, biting!
No pestilence exists in life
that causes so much human horror
as it does to those touched by woe.

    And why not, if good turns its back,
if even sun does not shine where woe lives,
if the tap that gïves water daily
is poisoned, if even bread tastes
of dry nothing in the mouth, and endless sea
instantaneously goes dry
if woe wants to drown in its harsh waves;
as for the arms of death that weary it,
even death recoils from woe!

    ¡Take pity, Lord! Bar the shadow
that keeps casting eternal night
over the light of faith, love, and hope!
Horrific shadow that obscures
shining stars in the heavens, that's made
new hell in this world, and a new world
where all courage loses its zeal
and all strength shatters without struggle,
where the long dark of pitilessness
bars every path that points forward.

    Kind Maker, with your potent breath,
dispel this horrible phantasm from us
and let woe come to an end;
enough already of of aches, of wretched
feeble flesh and of infallible death,
that torment and punish those sad ones who
having gone awry, live banished
from the exalted foyer for which they sigh!

There's no poet active in the nineteenth century, the twentieth, or our own twenty-first, who—to my knowledge—more clearly addresses depression as a women's and human health issue, as an issue that can be provoked—and we realize it in reading the poems that surround this one—by migration and precarity.

Disgracia was Rosalía's title. *Un*-grace. More than ill fortune, more than bad luck, *desgracia* is the suffering of a painful event, a loss of grace (and thus bears a tint of "sin"). Yet it is not our *disgrace*, and it is more than tribulation, for a mighty soul can vanquish tribulation *Desgracia* brings you so low; there is a causality, an economy at work. What we today call "depression," here I title, simply, *woe*. As an issue of intimate life it also involves the public sphere and Rosalía insists on this.

The poet's passionate social ire is evident in WOE, and the poem is no mere plaint, for even if depression touched her deeply (during the period she wrote these poems, there were political and familial and health setbacks), she was able to rise to speak, which many cannot. The struggle Rosalía de Castro touches and acknowledges is a wrenched hole in the social fabric that she does not evade.

Depression in her era had no pharmaceutical alleviation. Then, as today, women were more prone to it, or more prone to admit to it. It's no coincidence that the early anti-depressant Valium was known as 'Mother's Little Helpers.' From market entry in 1963 to the end of patent in 1985, it was a top-selling North American drug. Along with it, drugs like Quaalude, a sleeping potion, found their way into our bloodstream as anxiety-repressants. Some turned out to worsen depression and suicidal thoughts, further degrading lives. The World Health Organization (WHO) has predicted that by 2020, major depressive illness will be second only to heart disease as the world's leading cause of disability. In our time, the pharmacology of depression treatment is more sophisticated than in Rosalía de Castro's, but it still remains that depression, *desgracia*, is often an offshoot of societal precarity: economic precarity for sure, yes, but also pecarity tied to race, gender identity, culture.

   ¡And so! When your desire
most ardent is fulfilled,
my endless laugh will then be
        laughter just sad and dark.

        ———

   From my solitary corner
I'll look for you serenely,
while on heels of spring and summer
I'll see winter gain you all.
        There's be no winter sadder,
        more harsh and wild!

        ———

   As leaves drop from trees in autumn,
from your hearts will fall
bright illusions that you scatter over
        cemetery earth
in which our dead sleep mingled
        in forgetting's silence.

        ———

   Then from folds of dark shrouds
they'll appear before your very eyes,
sayyng: —I bet this wasn't what you sought
when you foolishly insulted heaven...
No doubt that wasn't it, unfateful ones,
        but... neither was it this...!
And in my corner I'll smile to myself
        a smile sad and dark.

The lust for accomplishment at all costs still leads to the cemetery ground....oh progress oh science oh capital!!!

Across mountains and fields,
paths and esplanades,
a single lonely dove flies out
alone from branch to branch.

Her poor chicks trail behind her,
thirsty and so frail,
for she's found not a bit of food
to put into their beaks.

She drags soiled plumage
that once was bright;
she drags, now scratched and sullied,
her weary broken wings.

Oh poor dove, once so white
who was once so cherished!
Where did your glów go?
Your lover, where did he wander?

Again the conversation here
is with silence; the tale's
told from the voice outside
the voice... is this *where
women's desire leads?*

An emigration song, seen through the condition of the woman and
children left behind... where? where's peace?

I CRAVE YOU, YOU CRAVE... *who?*...
—a variation in which we only hear one side of the dialogue, because....

   —The pretty grand dame
of peerless beauty,
where's she off to at this odd hour,
in a night so dark?
Where's she headed so intently?

———

   She's off through mud
in her silken slippers...
Through prickly görse the lady heads,
her husband left between fine sheets!
May Odin let him sleep soundly!

———

   Let him sleep, and my eyes will watch
the most gorgeous lady
I've seen in the world and ever will;
as gardener, I'll care for the rose
whose perfume's enjoyed by another.

———

   I'll care for it, night and day,
without rest or peace,
for neither of those are for me.
Body and soul, I won't hold back;
I'll devote myself fully.

———

   And even if she's not aware,
I know how much I care for her,
but such knowledge will be my end...
Fly, sweet dove; go, dear star,
someone valiant watches over you.

. . . .
. . . .

Where's she going? The hidden
door creaks open slowly...
The stitched silks murmur
as they swish down the path
that goes from fount to mill...

———

I can't see her, but she's there;
her sweet perfume reaches me,
I feel her footsteps,
and my heart, in aching
pleasure, leaps a beat.

———

Noble dame, pretty lady,
of all the hearts you cherish,
forgïve me, yes, forgïve me
if I follow t'you where you go:
don't you see you're in peril?

———

On such a stormy night,
who planted such desire in you?
You'd even splatter mud on roses...!
And in my heart I discern
that you've no blessed host to save you.

———

What if you meet the wandering souls?
What if the goblin beckons to you?
And fools you with its talk
and sets the table with its banquet
amid thunder and lightning?

———

You'll not go alone, despite yourself,
you'll not go alone as long as I breathe,
for it'd be against the Maker.
Lady, that One does not allow
people to seek out danger.

—

    Without you knowing that I follow,
I'll trail close behind you,
in case the devil tempts you.
And as long as it is not yet dawn
I will not leave you, my Lady.

—

    —Farewell… farewell, lady of beauty;
to give in to such bad ways!
It wasn't wandering souls who seized you,
you were spirited off by the devil.

—

    My soul's gripped by shadows…
Oh, crazy love…, crazy love ¡…!
That old saying sums it up:
I crave you, you crave ….

                another…….¿who?…

...*the woman addressed has no time for the speaker.*– There's a form of
stalking here, too, and again, a judgement on women's virtue, though
we know very well by now that "virtue" is a word used to police desire–

—¡Be brave! For though you're pliable as wax,
    we are in danger here;
on the other side, freedom awaits you
    no one here will grant you.
—Let's go, my Sir, where you wish,¡let's go!

   —So noble you are, my Love, and striving;
but you tremble like a trapped she-crow;
now Luck's brought us together we can
both flee, my treasured Love!
      —So let's flee, let's fleee!

     —Are you afraid, Love o'my life,
to be found in my arms
and that, in sharing love, we'll die?
—¡Oh, no! It's pure happiness.
    But let's leave… leave…
my steadfast Love… and farewell, peace and virtue!

Here too it is hinted that it is the woman who loses most in listening
to the entreaties of love: her "virtue" is abandoned.

But… to Rosalía.. the woman has desires too!

   The angels flew down
to where she was,
made her a bed
of placid wings,
and bore her away
in the silent night.
   When at dawn of day
the bell tolled,
and in the steeple high
the lark sang out,
the angels to each other,
their wings folded,
—¿Why, they marmured,
why wake her up?...

*Silence, again, is the
interlocutor, & the
woman finds peace
only in death...*

—Scared, I see the abyss
where I'm out walking now.
The heart is such a tyrant,
and it beats fierce for you, my love!
So I, unable to stop myself,
hear but one voice alone,
and where it wishes me to go,
unable to resist, I go…

—Today, at night, as all sleep,
through the window I will flee;
shadows will speed me onward…
Farewell, house of my birth!
  Honour I so did value,
sanctity of my home…
For love, I leave you all
and for all eternity!
  ¡Maker…! You'll condemn me;
and I deserve it, yes I know;
but… go on, condemn me,
I'll suffer it by his side!

The one-voice dialogue in which silence is cosmic interlocutor, a
Maker and deity.

This voice could be that of the woman in XIV or XV…

    —For life and for death
and forevermore
I asked you of God and God gave you me
for all eternity.
    —For life and for death
and forevermore,
I want to be yours and that you be
naturally Lord of me.
    —But she who wants this knows
she must have no dad, nor brothers,
nor man, if she's married,
nor children if she's mother.
    —What you say is shocking,
but I feel that it's true,
take me Lord for I'll go
wherever you want me to.
    —So come, for what is the world
to whoever has eternity?
Together we must live,
together they must bury us,
and our bodies here,
and our souls there,
God wills that in eternal union
they'll be forevermore.

. . . .
. . . .

    As does the serpent to the bird,
and sparrowhawk to the dove,
he pulled her from her nest
and never there will she return.

The same story? A dialogue in the form of a marriage vow that is then broken as the woman follows her desire...

XIX AT THE TOMB OF ENGLISH GENERAL
SIR JOHN MOORE
Fallen In Battle At Elviña (Corunna) 16 January 1809

To my friend Maria Bertorini, native of Wales
A Coruña, 1871[9]

How far away, so far, from those dark mists,
green pines, and churning waves
that saw his birth! From his paternal home,
sky of the land that lovingly caressed him,
from the places, oh, of his longïng, how far!....
They saw him fall under enemy blows
to never rise again, poor wretch!
To die as he did, upon foreign beaches,
die so young, abandon life
not yet done with life, still yearning!
To taste the fruit that could have been!
And instead of the wreath of laurels
that crowns the manly head of heroes,
to be lowered into the tomb silent and mute!

Oh white swans of the British Isles,
oh groves that border gallantly
along green banks of the bucolic rivers
and fresh fields where John once ran…!
If only his bitter sobbing sigh reaches you,
as with his last breath
he bids you farewell, with loving yearning,

---

[9]María Bertorini is the married name of María Margarita Jones, come from
Cheshire to Iria Flavia (near de Castro's home in Padrón) with her husband
Camilo Marcos Bertorini, Barcelona-born promoter of the first railway in
Galicia. Angueira suggests that the dedication points to a shared Celtic link
between peoples of the UK and those of Galicia. I think it points to a shared
link among women who were neighbours. As Angueira says, the poem sets
up a mausoleum of words for Moore, making him a younger man (he died
at 48). Corunna was the British name for A Coruña, appropriate for the
poem's English title. *(Again a migrancy addressed here…and England is
imaginary, Galicia real!)*

sending to you the last thoughts
that from his mind easily escaped;
with what mourning, with such unspeakable grief
with such unequalled strangeness we would
bid farewell! to he who so far away, so very far,
from his country, alone, was lowered to eternity.

And the greát seat, the stilled drapery
of the forever-abandoned bed;
the cold ash of the hearth without flame,
the soft carpet that loyally maintains
a visibre mark of the Dead man's foot,
the dog that awaits its absent master
and seeks him wandering down barren roads,
in the high grass of the overgrown lane
where once he did take solace in his walks,
the ever constant murmur of the fountain,
where he would go sit in fading afternoon…
How they will speak endlessly of Moore
in his own clipped and stilted language,
the eyes, oh, of those who wept for him!
And nevermore…., nevermore, oh sadness,
will he return to where they await him!
He went bravely, to do battle in glory.
He went! He went!… and did not return, for death
scythed him down there in foreign fields,
like the flower that falls where its own seed
will find no soil in which to root.

So you fell, poor John, far from the tomb
where you'd thought you'd rest with your own.
In foreign soil your bones still sleep
and those who loved you and still remember,
in gazing at the waves of the veiled Ocean,
say grieving, from your native beaches:
—He's out there, across that wild sea;
there he remains, perhaps, perhaps forever,
in a tomb where no one will weep, or cherish
the beloved ashes of the one we've lost…!
And sad winds and quiet breezes

so beloved by those dead who sleep far
from their native soil, come to refresh you
in summer's hot nights, and carry
you laments in a caress of wings,
soft sighs, loving echoes;
a teardrop still wet, that dampens
the dry stone of the cold mausoleum,
bringing wild perfumes from your country.

    But what a beautiful and unequalled abode
your mortal remains had luck to find!...
God did not wish for you,
noble stranger, an alien home...
There's no poet or dreaming spirit
who, on contemplating in autumn
the seä of dry yellowed leaves
that cöver your mausoleum with love,
who, on contemplating at fresh dawn
the smiling light of the month of May
that always comes in joy to visit you,
won't say: —Thus too when I die, that I might
lay in peace in this flowring garden,
close to the sea... far from graveyards!...
May you never hear, oh Moore,
bitter tears, nor whining prayers,
nor may other dead call to ask you in deepest night
to share the awkward sway of ghostly dances.
Only the gentle breath of the bud that opens,
of the flower that withers its last farewell,
crazy foments, childish laughter
of pretty children who come to hide
behind your white stone, unfrightened.
And, at times, ¡and often, I hope! you'll hear the sighs
of ardent love, that wind lifts up from
only God knows where... may they
keep you peerless company in your final home.
And the sea, the sea, wild sea that röars
a roar that rocks you where you are cradled,
lives at your side, comes to kíss the stones
of the loving ground that holds you in its love,

and around your resting place lets roses grow!...
Rest in peace, rest in peace, oh Moore!

   And you who love him, people of Albion,
watchful of your honour, rest eäsy.
Galician earth is noble earth—God has
granted it much beauty—; it knows how
to honour all who merit honour,
and honoured yes, as he merited, is Moore.
He is not lonely in his tomb; Galicians
watch with compassionate respect over
this foreigner whom traitorous death
kept far from his own, and who had to ask
of strangers a final haven.

   When you cross the sea's waves
to come to visit your brother,
lend to his tomb your ear's caress,
and if you feel the ashes moving,
and if you hear indefinable voices,
and if you hear what those voices say,
your soul will feel consoled.
He'll tell you that nowhere in the world
could he have found a better tomb
outside of England than this loving refuge!

A hymn to Galicia, dedicated to R's neighbour Marie. R writes Byronic ode: how better to address her neighbour than to adopt one of her native verseforms? An ode glorifies an individual or thing, an elegy mourns its loss–Moore was fitting less for elegy than for ode, as he is distant as a subject and his legacy is questionable. Many Galicians saw Moore's 1809 retreat to Coruña as abandonment and proof of English unreliability. He was chased by Napoleon's troops when he fled; but he left because he was outnumbered, and thought to take his troops away intsead of fighting (subjecting them to great suffering in the Galician winter). An early version of a Brexit? Here again, a conversation, dialogic: one-sided, for it is with the dead.

I

With what grace you sway
your body lithe
out on the dance floor
with that gallant beau,
just as the gentle alder
branches sway in north wind;
and leaves one upon another
yellow-tinged
keep falling, tangling
in your curled locks,
crowning you with sadness,
as withered, oh God in heaven,
as the sadness your own thoughts
settle in your soul…
It's that autumn's fleeting…
Winter's on its way!

But in the depths
of the pleasant valley, gentle
winds still quietly blow,
bringing perfumes from heaven.
Even now on lush banks
flecked with cling-peach blossoms
where the Miño River flows
majéstic and somnolent,
the sweet final sigh
of summer can be heard,
which lingers sleeping still
in rosemary and lavender,
just like a ray of hope
lingers in your heart.

II

But if there's one bad sign,
and bad sign it is indeed,

it's that speeding currents
never turn back.
¿What is it you hope for, when hope
pays you no mind?

Onward, woman,
bring your pilgrimàge to an end;
though you may not want to stop,
out there fierce hurricanes
and waves will snatch you
from your unlucky fate.

You've still got faith! You'll
have it, poor dear, in your ills;
you'll have it in the thorns
that come to torment you:
in the poisonous bile that
you'll drink without thirst;
in the hard and bitter bread
that will feed you.

Gentle waves never
turn back in the sea;
your stubborn destiny will never
be soothed by fortune,
nor will happiness revive you
with its sweet rest;
for only the sleep of death
lets the sad rest in peace.

So bring to a close
your triste pilgrimage,
for all born under a bad sign
are dogged by bad signs.
On wings of woe
your destiny flies,
and speeding currents
never turn back.

When abjection is invisible, the citystate and knowledge can endure, says Kristeva (Powers of Horror 84). By making abjection visible in her poems, Rosalía makes this continuity impossible: another repartition of the sensible is needed.

—Shush, oh winds of night;
shush, fountain of Serena,
for at the end of Trompas alley
        I want to hear who comes!

——

All the winds died down,
the fountain spilled more quietly,
and I saw that they came to bury
        her very heart.

——

Later I saw her still alive
in fields and in the meadows:
she'd gone looking for a tomb
        to give her earth.

——

She's not found one, and that's why
though her heart's gone dead
its gangrene, visible to us,
        glows yet.

and if that gangrene of the heart alive
yet
turns and tosses, touching us (silence is the interlocutor here too)

Some see black,
others white,
yet one and all
are out of joint.

I

—Be astute if you know how to:
avenge insults if you can;
        to one who dishes them at you, repay him;
but to one who never insults, do the same;
        for the morals of saints
don't always match the morals of men.

So a rough Galician mountaineer,
fed up with rancour and humiliation,
on his deathbed advised his son,
inheritor of his troubles and his name.

II

—Be innocent and always loyal,
        pardon whoever offends you,
do well each day by friend and foe,
and with door unlocked, attend without fear;
there's but one Maker and one morality that saves
        Eve's sad offspring.

This the poor widow
of the mountaineer, dying in poverty,
resignedly said to her son,…
and to her Maker she gave up the ghost, serene.

III

    And he presided over her
all alone in his sighs and tears;
no priest in those parts would give
a charity burial to the poor.
    In a corner of the yard,
where prickly nettles grew,
without cross, sign or gravestone,
she lay lost and laid to rest,
and her son sad and lonely,
turned back in anger to his empty home.
    —My Dad advised me one way, he thought,
and my Mom another;
and though she was saintly and of good conscience,
he had experience and knowledge in spades.
      I am son of both….
so I'll cleave my legacy in two:
My mother: do well to those who do you well,
My father: your very bones demand revenge.

One afternoon out in Castile,
the sun beat down as it had always done,
beaming on that desert.

Clear, burning, and insolent,
excuse me, but it's no way to act,
charring folks like that,

and joyfully shrivelling
each poor simple plant,
each fountain, each parched river.

One afternoon, oh what sadness,
the sun attacked me in its perfidy,
seeing me so hopeful!

Where's it going to stop?
I thought, gazing at sky
so as to lift my eyes from earth.

Because the sky was, oh yes,
more or less as blue
as ours in Galicia.

But the earth, good Grief!
Lord, is it possible
that you made it?

But why do I find it strange
since in all of your acts
you never act badly...

You created those sad plains,
but you did it, clement Maker,
just for Castilians.

¡Ah! Every dove has its nest,
every rabbit its burrow,
every soul its soulmate.

That's what I intoned
that afternoon, memory
of dark melancholy.

And meanwhile, I gazed
across the flat expanse of plain,
at earth that was blanching;

at the greát weary pinewood,
its dark stain without end;
at the village, scorched in colour.

And between soil and sky,
the wind was stirring
clouds of thick dust.

Desert's true image,
with desert's burning breath,
¡desert's hot courage!

In the distance, the muletrain passed,
the herd of bulls drew closer,
the ailing sheep bawled.

And on scorched bramble,
fleeing the ardent sun,
a small bird rested.

Oh my, its tiny anxiety!
Sadness weighed me down,
as if I were buried alive.

Memories of beautiful land,
calm with freshness,
ached in my weeping soul.

While the parched river
shrouded in fetid fogs,
provokes fevers, provokes chills.

Suddenly I heard a song,
a song that moved me
till it took my breath away.

It was a Galician melody,
it was the *alalá*... that made
my heart leap.

With a strange rhythm:
sweet, as if well loved;
savage, as if in pain!

Caked in sweät and dust,
scythes on shoulders,
through those desert fields

a team of harvesters came...
And it was they, they, were
the charmed bearers of song!

¡Farewell, scorched pines!
¡Farewell, sun-grilled soils
and desolate headlands!

I closed my eyes and saw...:
saw freshets, meadows, and plains
spread at my feet.

When I opened them again,
dying of yearning,
I broke into tears.

And could not stop crying
until from Castile
I was borne away.

They bore me away so that in Castile
they'd not have to bury me.

To be in a world of exile and hear the lilt of the Galician language!

XXIV

Frigíd months of winter
that I love with all my heart,
months of icy rivers
and sweet love of the hearth.
    Months of storms,
where pain does find its bower
as it assails young folk
and cuts them down in flower.
    It's home and back in autumn
that causes leaves to sway,
I laid down to sleep in leaf-fall
so as to dream my being away.
    And when the pretty sunlight
of April smiles again,
may it shine upon my rest,
and no more my suffering.

XXV

I

It was in the month of May,
in the month of love, of plants and flowers,
month of suave prefumes
and transparent colours.
Of morning trills of little birds,
of fresh and candid dawns,
of fleeting clouds,
of afternoons a-smile and golden.
When the sea is blue, the sky serene
like a sleeping baby,
rivers gentle, high the stars,
more faded is the moon,
yet also more beautiful,
with its own peerless grace.
It was, in short, a time when all in this life
smiled on mortals with the happy, splendid
virginal smile of spring
that invites all to love and be lucky.

Invites all…oh! If only fate
could máke it so;
for there's one who, cloaked in the dark
of his own sadness,
sees only, in lovely spring,
in warming sun and in the rose
glistening with fresh dew of morning,
a sad bad omen that awakens
thoughts of mourning and misfortune.

II[10]

It was a morning in the month of May
on which it seemed the angels sang,
while breezes gently moaned
in a lament so loving;
and the rivulet trickling past the curtain
lightly murmured who knows what,
and the flight of restless swallows
who twittered in the air,
at the sight of wise clouds
foretold adventures and pleasures.
Morning of enchantments,
just what the spirit craves
as it waits and trusts;
morning that calls every being
to pleasure and joy,
apart from the sad soul
that in his very being knows not
what it is to feel relief and calm,
where sweet pleasure starts,
where the cruelty of pain ends.

III

Oh kind guardian angel, you
who slowly bat pale wings
around the afflicted spirit,
to touch it with blessed consolings
you bear us from the infinite,
where oh where have you been,
and why in such dark sorrow

---

[10]Many lines in this section end in Galician with past imperfect verbs, which
preclude closure. There's a rhythm of ongoingness into the space beyond
the line end. It is a past tense that anticipates. In English, the rhythms of the
past imperfect do not offer that same movement, as the imperfect requires
two words, a distraction. So something of the Rosalian rhythm goes missing
here, something of that part of meaning that is provoked by formal qualities.

did you leave that one sad soul?
Faith, hope, charity,
soürce of eternal beatitudes,
from luckier regions, you
come to calm our bitterness...
where are you, doing what?
When the one who places trust in you,
struggling alone in worried agony,
orphan, calls you without response?

IV

Among all those he insistently hated,
among all who he loved spitefully,
a sad one condemned to hard fate
plunged his gaze into the wild Cantabrian surf
wondering if
in such a deep tomb
the huge space of another world might be visibre.
And with adamant spirit,
so as to touch the clear liquid
he raced in a dizzying run
as if in the lure of the mysterious abyss
a strange power leads him to death.

And he said:—Farewell, life! Farewell, torment,
that with slow martyrdom
robs even my dreams of hope!
As for my misfortune,
I'll breák the grip of its strong arm
to go where there is no pain, or change,
where worry is buried in repose.
And you, evil passion loosed in me
you were my Maker and my punishment,
if you still want to kill me, die with me!

The sad one stopped, and fearsome
huge waves with manes of foam
twisted back upon the sands,

inciting the poor wretch
to end the battle
that had started in his breast.

     But a soft sound
suddenly found the perturbed ear
of that unlucky chump…
And he listened astounded to
an invisible being whose alluring talk
in soft and celestial melody
suavely and gently told him:

     —Stop right there at your life's
shore, cowardly sentinel;
¡don't think that by fleeing the present
you'll pull the veil from eternity!
Try to take the path of life
between the roses and the bile;
don't leap into your tomb
before the Maker asks it of you.
No offspring of Eve is ever freed
finally from their pain
until death comes of its own accord.
After having crossed
the huge deserts of the infinite,
you'd return to the world in spirit
to suffer, and pay for your crime.
By day and night,
without rest or release
you'd find yourself stuck to that breast
where the ungrateful heart beats
not for you but for the sake of repetition.
And in that thought
with implacable clarity you'd read
treacherous betrayal, bitter oblivion
unhidden by veils or tricks.

—Oh G/ºd, all-powerful Maker!
What horrific torment!

—No one can reverse the power of destiny
miserable or benign;
nor is it easy for anyone
to alter their fate.
Only those who wait and hope will triumph…
So get back to life and wait resigned.

　　And he turned to live, repented
though sad and hurt
was that poor wretch:
he asked G/d's pardon for his sin,
and G-d, compassionate,
gave him blessed peace and sweet oblivion.

"If the Law is in the Other, my fate is neither power nor desire, it is the fate of an estranged person; my fate is death." Julia Kristeva, *Powers of Horror*, 87

Here Rosalia's dialogue is with the silent sufferer, whose dialogue in turn is with the cosmos....

WHAT'S UP?

    Always a plaintive ¡oh!, a qualm,
a desire, an anguish, an ache...
At times it's a star that dazzles,
at others it's a ray of sun;
it's the leaves that fall from trees,
then it's flowers that burst in fields,
        and it's the wind that moans;
        and it's the cold, and heat...
And it's neither wind nor sun, nor is it cold;
        it's not..., it's just
the soul assailed, poet and sensitive,
        lashed by disappointment
        railing at everything.

—You, charming and white as snow,
    and prettiest of all among the best;
you, around whom men buzz, flitting
as bees do toward a rose
(guys who, and it's the same for women,
are capable of every betrayal);
you never love, but are loveable;
you never gïve forth, they gïve forth to you;
if they wound you, my beloved, laugh;
if they cheat you, my love, don't cry.
The age of Corinne[11] is clearly long gone,
    and just as you suffer now
      when you have to bite your tongue,
      you'll just rage later, when you can.
—Rage? you say. That sounds untrue!
    —Yes, yes, rage loudly;
for the needle itch of rage
is the tasty sauce of passion.
What would happen to poor stomachs, oh god!,
    without absinthe?
    And as for the heart these days,
where'd it be without rage, my love?

---

[11] A reference to Madame de Staël's *Corinne, Or Italy* (1807)

(Serenade at Dusk)

Ventura Ruiz de Aguilera, **tr.** from Spanish by Rosalía de Castro

tr. from Galician by EM, without rhyme. *–A mirror of a mirror, a mise en abyme–*

※   ※   ※

November heaved a sigh
as tired and alone I took a seat
beneath the crumbling wall,
ancient rampart and village border.

Through a house of cracks
left agape by time to lizards,
today the salamander watches
gazing coldly at the ravages around it.

Nasty and pale,
creeping nettle and sickly sour radish,
the many fronds moán
when the wind moves them.

Capstones crown
the wrecked portal of the chapel
that stands in the churchyard,
skeleton in the dust of altars.

Already at the sacred hearth
no mother kindles fire while praying,
and from soot-dark stones
wind has long swept the ashes;

and from the ancient arches
and columns, stones jar loose and fall
just as teardrops do
from inconsolable sad eyes.

How the rotting leaves
fall from the branch where they were born,
rubble left from life that
once charmed these quiet woods.

And the river seems
almost dried up its pebbled bed,
miserable relic of a channel
once clean, copious, serene!

How the hills are aflame
in autumn sun as light wanes,
while shadowy the night
quietly surprises the valley.

The tolling in the distance
of a bell sighing prayers:
the dying afternoon

says its fond farewell to religion.
    And the little owl hovering
also cries its chill predictions,
like one dead without tomb,
who wanders a graveyard's edge.
    As its wings beat,
its voice awakens sleepy echoes,
and seems to resound
behind what passes pensive and austere:
    the mysterious roár
of visions marshalled by fears,
pale skeletons screaping long shrouds
darkly across the ground.
    Oh may the populace waken
from its eternal repose,
exhausted pilgrims
finding new energy in rest.
    They take up their trek again
at the sweet dawn of serene day,
its splendid light dressed
modestly in a veil of cloud.
    But the spell ends,
a moment later; thus the remains
of mortal illusions fill
the heart with soulful feeling.
    And once again from the wall
stones crumble and gïve way,
and the leaves to this cadence
keep falling from yellow trees,
    just as teardrops
fall from sad and inconsolable eyes
to the rubble left from life that
once charmed these quiet woods.
    All things pass; shadow
always follows on the light of clear sky
and old age expires.
Youth is, oh, but fleeting memöry.
    You alone do not perish,
oh, spirit that sighs in its cell!
But death's compassionate hand
will finally break your chains.
    The frale vase of your immortal essence
now in pieces will remain,
and rising into air, it
will go seek out eternal love.

> To the land you'd lost,
> you'll fly up gently from the soil
> that your wings brushed
> when you fell to desert from the world.
> ¡There, oh! you recall it sadly,
> just as a banished wretch recalls
> her homeland and its blue skies
> from the banks of foreign rivers.

※   ※   ※

In translating into minority idiom from the hegemonic (it is still more usual to translate the other way), Rosalía has Ruiz de Aguilera's view of Galicia—as crumbling to ruins—confront the vitality of the Galician language. To Rosalía, translation is both intimate (one of HER poems), and conversation (a response to VRdA). Her version of his poem nabs his florid romanticism very well (oh Wordsworth or Byron on ruins); the tone is not the straight-ahead tone or music of her own work. Intriguing as well how she bookends the translation with poems of her own: one that ends with RAGE and one that starts with the SQUEAL of a cart. These too are sonic commentaries on Ruiz de Aguilera and his sighing ruins!

It is RdC's translation that survives today in the culture, not VRdA's original.

Squeal of carts from Ponte,
sad bells from Herbón;
when I hear you, my heart-
strings snap.

———

Onion sellers who come and go
along the road through Adina,
when you pass the burial ground
go gently and slowly.

———

I know it's said the dead don't hear,
but when I go speak to my own dead,
I'm certain that, though silent,
they hear my grief intoned.

With powerful minimalist language gestures, Rosalía says so much
more than the florid Aguilera!

With the deadly blade
sunk in my chest,
my spirit in shadow
and body in muck
darker than death,
than the lowest of earth,
clots of blood
I was weeping.

Suddenly in the thick
of brown fog
with rare harmony
arose a tune...
How fresh and sweet,
how light and strange
it resounded in the hidden
caverns of the sands!

My aches were calmed
as thirst is with water,
as the poor parched one
at the fountain finds peace.
Trapped in my eyes
the tears remained,
while immobile and
suspenseful, I listened.

From times remote,
from distant ages,
from serene nights
forever past,
that singing brought me
so many memories,
not dead... sleeping,
who knows in what tombs!

I thought I'd heard it
in the fields of Italy,
where perhaps I was queen,
perhaps but a slave,
on the shores of the Bosphorus,
at the castle window…
But deep love always
I felt in my soul.

What strange dreams
were stirred in me,
by the unknown music
of such mellifluous song?
Of former lives,
that in remembering
calmed the aches
of present cares?

¿Who can say?
Mysteries of fragile
human nature,
no one can explain;
I only know that, feeling
consolation in my soul,
I loved from that moment
the mandolin's tune.

How music brings us, in the echo of an instrument, out of our lives and into…
Just as those with stroke damage can dance to music, and those with dementia
can still sing, our human brain—science shows—responds to music even when
broken.

Pallid virgins with candid faces,
Hallowed gents with unfurrowed brows,
        noble matrons,
        austere nuns,
and even those whose soles seem never
        to have touched
        the muck of earth,
in their consciences, hidden, who knows
        how defiled they are?

        ——

        But sure as there's wide rivers,
        and immense seas,
        and lakes unprobed
and torrents that uproot griefs,
in all spheres of this world
        there's no water washes
        a defiled conscience clean;
        and those that defile themselves
        defiled they remain.
They'll only come clean with the copious tears
        of repentance!

Some rich folk try to sink the poor,
and as for the poor, it's the greát they sink,
        all to puff themselves up,
        and act proud till they die.
Vanity, how you waltz amid men,
right till the gates of death open!
        But once they're lowered into the hole,
        each and all are equals;
        dust turns to dust
        and with it, pride.

Hurry, Álvaro of Anido,
live a lot in a little time,
goad your horse
and in goading it, burst it.
¿What's one noble horse?
¿What're two or three hundred?
What counts, Álvaro Anido,
        is arriving early.

Run from one end to another,
map all the dark caves,
climb up on the locomotive,
rise up in dirigibles,
and scuttle like a crab
over the breadth of the void:
you're a man, Álvaro, you'll give out,
        running and running.[12]

---

[12]Iria Flavia, near Padrón where de Castro lived, was home to the Bertorinis and their son-in-law John Trulock, two of the English families that brought and promoted the first railway in Galicia (1873). Locomotives would have been a potent symbol of "progress" heard nearby, as de Castro finished this book. And the new railway cut off direct access to the sea. Our poet is sceptical of the good in speeding over the surface past everything.

—You claim that marriage
is blessed and good. So be it,
but Saint Anthony[13] never wed,
though even the devil
tried to get him to do it.

———

They wore hairshirts plural, yes;
and did heaps of penance;
but I notice that no saint wished
to shoulder the heavy cross
of the married.

———

Not even the holy fathers,
of whose scriptures we have many,
along with all their hallelujahs,
wanted to sink their holy feet
into the muck of marriage.

———

From every angle,
matrimony, you're a noose;
you're a temptation to hell,
but I'll get married..., for winter's coming...
I need someone to warm my feet!

---

[13]St. Anthony of Padua is patron of marriages and reconciliation of couples. His feast day is in June, which, even in North America today, is considered a month of marriages. This is an anti-clerical poem in that makes light of the holiness of wedlock, finding but one good reason for getting married: warmth for cold feet!

Now hair of black,
much later hair of grey;
now pearly whites,
tomorrow yellowed incisors;
today cheeks all rosy,
tomorrow wrinkled leather.
Black death, dark death,
cure for aches and folly,
¿why don't you just slay us grrls
so that the years can't do it?

XXXVI

—May you end up, by God,
writhing like a snake in sand;
may the water you go to drink
clog your mouth with weeds.
May you beg and never find
rest, peace, or protection;
and even dead with hunger,
may you end up at a wall.
—Curse, mouth, curse
while I'm heading down the road:
the curses of fallen women
never work on soldiers.

This poem, in my translation, was published in a 2016 book beside a photo of a WWI soldier charming a woman in France through a doorway…. ah but soldiers! Don't they always leave?

I've a sickness incurable,
since I was born,
and this inimical sickness
will send me to the grave.

———

Folk healers, surgeóns,
medical doctors...
for this infirmity of mine,
there's no remedy among humans.

———

So stop turning pages
with diligence or with none;
in the books of your sciençe,
for me you'll find nothing.

———

You have your doubts? There's none
in what I'm saying, doctors;
even if you hate to hear it, it's bitterness
no syrup sweetens.

———

You're upset because you think
I overstate my case?
Well have a go then..., all hands to work:
try and cure me, friends.

———

My sickness and my suffering
are nothing but my heart.
Dig it out of me without flinching!
Then... ¡make me live!

Pleasure, if you've scabies, distracts from the itch;
without it, the itch wins over;
yet, to ring true, affliction
has to ache deeply.
There's no suffrance in bleeding tears
at the feet of your beloved.
To live far from him, and forgotten,
this, yes, is truly rótten!

—It's true any person can
be bad or good;
but to come from solid stock
is better, if you would.
    Despite your shiftless ma and pa,
today you're a Marquis;
even so, all said and done,
we return to the source, when we flee.
    Dog born of a fox,
that they claim is now loyal:
if it's not killing chickens
it's because it's been foiled.

    So sang a blind bard
at the Harvest fair,
making listeners snicker
as if the story were rare.
    And they peered at each other
as if meaning to say:
—Scratch your own ïtch, bub;
I don't itch, no way.

XL

You write some verses and... *what verses!*
Never seen their ilk before:
each verse armed with gravel,
knuckledusters every one,
as if they're made for thwacking
the reader in the nose.

You write some verses and... *what verses!*
Never seen their ilk before:
each verse armed with gravel,
knucklebusters you've composed
as if they've got their dukes up
to thwack the reader in the nose!

An echo here of the medieval cantigas of scorn and slander....

A child trembled in the damp portal...
Hunger and cold
mark his angélic face
still pretty, but worn and dull.

Ragged and shoeless, on the stones
his poor wee feet were
split by the ice of winter.
He rests tentatively;
they look as if cut by blades
of razor wire.

Like dog without hayrick or master,
whom all despise,
he hides trembling in a corner
under the stairs.
As a lily droops when it withers,
the golden-haired innocent
also droops, faint with hunger,
and rests his face on the stones.

And as he sleeps,
sad image of pain and poverty,
they press past him to adore the Most High.
What Pharisees, the exalted of the earth;
even seeing the orphanhood of the innocent
does not calm
the greedy thirst of the rich.
Anguish oppresses my heart,
¡Maker! God of Heaven!
Why are their souls so dark and hard?
Why are there orphans on earth, bountiful Maker?

But it's not in vain that the book of
mysteries stays sealed...
Glory, power and happiness pass...
...All on this earth passes. *We hope!*

And so ends the book of variations... the voices of others, the plaints, the injustices, the treatment of women by men... it all ends with *hope*. Hope that it will pass. And to that hope is yoked a "we," the *we of the missing people.*

On green riverbanks, on shimmering beaches
and in the rough cliffs of our towering sea,
there are eerie folksongs, of spells unknown,
that only with us share their playful plea.

———

In the loving shade of our oakwoods,
and in our fresh meadows of vivid splendoúr,
and in the murmur of springs, there are cherished spirits,
that offer loving words to those born here.

———

And in our mountains and in these our skies,
as long as there's life here, as long as being exists,
there are bright suave colours, of humid transparency,
of uncertain vagary, that to us alone gïve bliss.

———

You who were born on different shores,
who are warmed by the flame of a living glare,
and who need a burning sun to live,
hush, if the charms of our home you don't share,
just as we, not seeing those of yours, go quiet.

Still stung by exile on the dry plains of Castile, and by disparagement
there of Galicians by Castilians. But... aren't we *all* earthbound?

My sweet abode, my hearth,
      you're worth more to me
than your weight in gold.

    From Santiago to Padrón,
I came in driving rain,
bare-legged and shoeless,
without dinner or breákfast.
On the road I spotted
rich things to buy,
and although I wanted them
I had no way to pay.
From restaurants rose aromas
of tasty things,
but those who lack money
have to walk on by.
I arrived at my house
exhausted from walking,
I didn't have a crumb there
on which to sup.
My sight was fading,
it was hard to hang on.
I went to a neighbour's house
that was full to the rafters;
I begged a little cornbread
and he wouldn't lend.
Tears fell from me
I was so ashamed.
I returned to my wee house
lit up by the moon;
I lookd in every crevice
to see what I could find:
I found some flour dust,
a small fistful was all,
at the bottom of the bread-bin
and gave praise to Gdd.
I wanted to light the fire,
but had no wood to burn.
I went to ask an old woman;
all she would share

was a stick of green bramble
to drive me round the bend.
I was sad as night
from crying just to cry;
I nabbed a fist of straw,
from my mattress it came;
I seached the whole stable
praying the whole while,
and saw a few bits of kindling
and ferns, thanks to G/d.
Miraculous Saint Anthony,
the home fire's alight!
I put the pot on the flame
with water to heat,
while I scratched
in the ashes, I saw the glint:
¡a lucky penny!
¡Oh Virgin of Pilar!
Out I ran quickly
and bought some salt,
happier than at Christmas
I returned to my yard,
and in my garden plot
I spied some cabbage leaves.
With a little old lard
that I'd wisely saved,
and with the fine flour,
I had enough to dine.
I made a glorious brotth
as tasty as the sea;
made a few dumplings
that were something to envy;
after I had eaten up
I said another prayer;
and after having prayed
I hung up my wet clothes,
for not a single thread was dry
I'd been soaked so bad.
And while they were drying,
I broke out in song

so that they'd hear me
everywhere:

My hearth, my home,
        to me you're worth more
than your weight in gold.

To not be alone on this earth, to have a home: *thinking the Nelson Eddy song (QR code on page 23) that was part of my own childhood.* St. Anthony, as noted earlier, is the patron of marriage; the narrator thanks him for she's married... to her home! The Virgin of Pilar, for her part, made a miraculous appearance in Spain in 40 C.E. while she was in Jerusalem, an instance of bilocation! Rosalía's more secular narrator associates this Virgin with the miraculous appearance of a penny far from its home. *Much more useful!*

Colour of lead, the clouds pile up;
the waves of the sea turn slow;
and roaring with a frightful sound
      the hurricane shows.

———

How heavy is the sky and sad;
¡how dark, how black it's turning!
We'll light the vigil candle,
      against the storm.

———

Riding on the wings of angels,
sent by the Almighty they'll race:
the lightning bolts that frighten evil
      with their flashing.

———

We'll burn nine leaves of olive,
to keep all evil away,
and to free us from the bolts of light
      that kill us.

———

The Trisagion prayer we all chorus,
bow down and adore our Maker;
for if it thunders, it's that we're reminded
      G/d's greát and immortal.

———

¡Holy, holy! They say to each other
      children and mother;
All, no, for one, prideful and irrascible,
      won't pray.

———

But the heavens drown in thunder
and blind lightning's glow.
Oh what a night! What terrible night
        of storms!

        ———

    The Almighty's irate… ¡Bow down!
Oh, wicked of the earth, tremble!
Whoever survives this night alive
        will tell the tale.

        ———
        ———

    —Mother, the tawny cow
shakes in her stall beside you.
Do you think her a sinner?
Will a bolt of lightning kill her?

        ———

    —It's not her who sinned,
you lousy Christian, it's you,
you've been an unrepentant sinner
from the minute you were born.

        ———

    —And the poor tawny cow
pays, I asked, for my sinning?
—You pay! With her dead,
tell me, what will you eat?

IV ¡POOR WOMAN SO DEAF…!
–*One of my Rosalía de Castro favourites*–

—There atop the mountain,
smoke rises from the chimneys…
Courage, old creaky body!
Carry me there, legs.
Slowly, ever so slowly,
stop here, sit there,
you'll get there, Joanie,
up where home fires are lit.
Hail Creátor, holy Virgin!
today, maybe… maybe… perhaps…
you'll have seven mugs
of good broth, to eat for supper,
and a bread chunk with pork
or salt-pressed sardines,
for the mountaineers are folk
who gïve freely, when they gïve.
After that, you'll warm at a blaze
big as a bonfire,
and when you're warmed well,
to sleep… right till morning!

And the old woman climbed
the steeps of the Sea of Sheep,
one eye on the ground,
the other on smoking chimneys.

All the while, afternoon sun
was setting in the pines,
and it lights the shady forests
with sad rays.
From Anxos the gay valley
shows off its green mantle
there in the peaceful dell
where soft breezes swirl.
Here spring, there creek,
water glittering in the grasses,

golden, as the last
ray of sun rests there.
Quiet, gentle calm
reigns high and low;
night comes quietly,
gently, starless.
Not a single light
glows in the firmament, for thick
fog rides out
across ethereal plains.
It starts to drizzle, dark
all around, even the familiar
is hardly recognizable,
neither road nor path.
But regardless,
the brave are truly brave,
and the old woman climbs up, up
the steeps of Sheepy Sea,
one eye on the ground,
the other on the houses smoking,
for a light glow-ed there,
and she heads to it
murmuring: —Upward, Joanie:
there's a feast ahead or I'm a fool.

    Experience teaches all,
and she had long experience;
that's why she wasn't wrong to think
that up there a feast awaited.

    Oak burned in the fire,
and around the hearth sat
girls with joyful eyes,
grandmas with long white locks,
old gals who roll sleeves
and clack the castanets,
the godchildren of the house
from all over the village,
and friends and in-laws,
cousins and other relations

all together, and even the priest
and the veterinary surgeon.
A blind man with hurdy-gurdy
alongside a blind woman
who sure can play tambourine
and make castanets chatter;
an armless man, a gimp, a madwoman
and other poor folk, all squished
on a bench for ten aside the hearth,
so jammed in none more could fit
though a few more hovered.
All arriving, arriving,
all sniffing out a party,
and no one was sent away
by the rich mountaineer's wife;
for there's plenty for all, today
they were cooking fresh meat,
heaps of it, and making
cauldrons of congee.
A sheep was butchered, big
as a bull, and a calf
large as a cow, and plump
as a little sow.
The wine flows, cinammon-
hued wine of the Ribeiro;
and for the riffräff
there's also local slosh,
on the tart side but bracing
and scrumptious as strawberries.
An ovenful of white cornbreäd
bakes, gold-topped, mixed with rye
and a little bit of butter.
This broa is as rich as cake,
you can't get enough of it;
it's even more savoury
than the specially chosen loaves
lugged in triple baskets from Santiago
by the bakerwomen.
In short, there was food all over,
and the wine gladdened

folks so much that dark sadness
went wild with envy.
The poor folks who'd come there
to find warmth and table,
told yarns that made all laugh,
all the lasses and grandmas,
some in verse, some in prose,
and they spoke in every language,
goading each other
to create even better couplets.
But the hurdy-gurdy player wins
with help from his companion,
both boosted by the white wine
that whet their throats.

    —Hail to our blind bards!
folk shouted from time to time
and the bard yelled louder:
—¡Bravo gents! ¡Bravo ladies!
especially the prettiest one
who just gave me a hug.
¡Woo-woo-woot! And he whoops
until the very stones were deafened,
and the blind woman shook the tambourine,
the blind man touched the keys,
and to the beat of zong, zong
the girls danced up a storm.
And the poor folk said, adding
fuel to the fire: —¡What a party!
No need to wander outside today
on an empty gut!
And they grin and stare
at the bales of fresh straw,
where they'll sleep all warm
like cracklings in broth,
while the wind wails outside
and dogs howl on the ranges.

    Now almost midnight,
it's time to start wrestling,

the boys with the girls,
marshalling their forces
and basking in compliments,
end up on the floor.
If you could see how strong
the girls are in the fray!
They give the boys a start
with their tiny gripped hands!

    —One's down alreády… it's a man…
She won, she won!
Yay for the pretty lass!
Yay for girl mountaineers!
Yay for them, they sure can wrestle!
—¡She cheated! he answers
in shame. —I was trapped, coz if not,
a hundred like her couldn't beat me.
—What kind of trap was it… for bats…?
I beat you…
        —No.
                —Yes.
                        —¡You beat me!

And in the fervour was heard:
¡Tap! ¡tap! ¡tap!, the sound of a stone
on the door.
                  —Who's that? they asked.
—I'm a poor old woman
who's lost on this mountain…,
she responded, her voice in a tremour.
Won't you shelter me a bit,
for it's raining and thundering?
—May G/d keep you; it's alreády late,
there's no room, they answered.
—What'd you say, ma'am? I'm deaf
as a capstone… my dear.
Open the door, and may the On High
bless you…
                —Poor old woman…
a little further on, not far at all,

there's more doors; go knock there.
—What'd you say, dear lady? Look
it's a wild night out here
and I'm scared the wolves
will eat me…

       —Goosh almighty! As if!
There're no wolves here, go on, go on,
God keep you, there's another village
close.

       —What'd you say, ma'am?
—Off you go, don't be stubborn,
there's no room here
for rich or poor, ¡yeáh!
—Whazzat, my dear? I'm deaf,
I can't hear even earsplitting noise.
Brrrrrr, it's cold, my lady!
You who are so charitable,
lët me in, and I'll go rest
in the stable with the animals.
Brrrr…. I'm dying of cold!
¡argh! ¡aughoaua! ¡argh! ¡aughoaua!
What a cough…, Gdd help me…, ¡brrr!
I can't take it!

       —Okay, come in,
and if you've nowhere to sit
the horse trough will have to do;
said the lady, who had
a heart of butter.
—God bless you, sweet lady!
You'll find reward
in heaven… Open, my jewel,
the old woman quickly exclaimed.
—What, she's not deaf, she heard!
they said from inside, while
pulling the bolt back
from the door.

       —Whazt, my dear?
I didn't hear a thing, I'm
just sensitive, that's all…

       —Oh I'll just bet

you're not lying... Come, come,
get inside...
                    —Blessed and good
night to you, my dear sirs...
¡Jeez, they're still partying,
it's jammed in here!
They'll still be here in a year, I wager.
God bless them all... the Lawrd
gave them fistfuls of luck
and there you go...
                    —Amen, amen!
Find a spot at the fire
and warm yourself up...
                    —Whatz you say?
I'm deaf as a stone,
and haven't had a crumb
since last night, and in my veins
my blood's stockstill
with cold...
                    And while
she said this, she drew close
to the fire so companionable
with the other wretches, and squeezed
in their midst, men and women all.
She jumped over the blind man,
and say what you like,
still shaking with cold
and deaf as a stone,
to hear her say it, she grabbed
the best spot, with greát humility,
and the fire flared warm where
she sat.
                    —Ay, old woman!
You're not the only one
here— ¡what a pushy
broad! another wretch told her
with a face to rob milk
from babies. —Whazt, my boy?
(smiling she replied,
settling in more cozily)

156

as for me, like it or not
I look after my own; in heaven
the Maker can take care of me…
                    —¡Bosh! it seems
you're trying to mock us folk…
—Phht, what's with that decrepit Judas!
She even looks like a poker.
—If I'd like a pint, my dear?
If they'd gïve me one, I'd just
sip at it once in awhile,
for I'm parched with thirst,
and hunger, and cold…
                    —Howl on,
dog! Never saw a deaf woman
so skinny and sneaky.
Is she kit of some fox?
—Is she grabbing at a bone? They
just wanted to kid her. ¡My Gawd!
But hunger was stárk in her;
—Just bring me what's left
sitting charred in the fire,
and I'll set to gnawing it
with the one fang I've got left.

    All laughed at her answer
and… —Though G/d wouldn't credit me,
said the blind bard, that deaf woman
knows more than I do, I say.
—She deserves bread and sop
and I'll gïve it her, old dear,
because I always love wisdom
wherever it appears.
—Eat your fill! Here's a chunk
and some wine; drink,
drink on my tab
to the heálth of mountain lasses,
said the hostess, and passed a plate
heaped high with tripe
to the wretch; and wine, and as much
white bread as she wanted; she stuffed

157

herself until her belly was tight
as a tambourine. She's nearly
bursting... but she battled
back, and didn't even
crack, and by the next day
she could waddle bent over.

    —Take it easy, said the hostess
when she left. Just saying:
don't come back here
as long as you're deaf.
—What'za say, my dearest?
the old woman responded laughing.
I'm deaf as a brick;
even if you split my head open, I can't hear.

*Many cultures have tales about the craftiness of the wanderer damned to
internal migration, who does not cross borders but meets one at every doorsill.
This woman is bound to her own earth, an internal migrant. And gifted! The
gift of life is one she has seized. Not as possession but as what is proper to her...*

Thinking Agnès Varda, and her *Sans toi ni loi...*

Jack's fetching wood on the mountain,
Jack's outside weaving baskets,
Jack's off to trim vines,
Jack's spredding manure,
and lugs the bellows to the mill,
and hauls dung to the stable,
and treks to the fountain for water,
and brings the kiddies to mass,
and makes beds and soup...
Jack, in short, is a Jack so complete:
the kind every woman
wants at least one of.
But look as she might for Jack
she almost always ends up with Juan (Don).

Then there's Jill, lucky Jill,
the wife of Jack we've just met,
while her husband works
she dangles toes in the creek,
picks lice off the cat,
combs her long hair,
tosses corn to the hens,
gossips with the priest's brother,
finds eggs in the nest,
peeks into the orchard,
licks cream off the milk,
and if she can, tosses back a pint
with her pal, who brings it
hidden under her apron.
And when Jack at night
comes home tired and hungry,
she awaits him in the sheets,
and when she sees him, murmurs:

—For Gawd's sake, cut the racket,
I'm a total wreck.
—What's wrong, my sweet woman?

—What's wrong? Putting kids to bed,
and this womb gnaws in me
like a dog's gnawing a bone,
and at the end I'm fit only
for the burial ground…
—Oh, my Jill, take a sip
of the herb liqueur I have here,
and sleep, sweet woman,
while the kids are abed.

    And his eyes brim with tears
when Jack sees what's before him;
but don't you fear, in every thousand
there's just one angel amid all the devils;
there's just one tormented
for every thousand who cause pain.

Jack (the earthbound), says Rosalía, is an exception to the odds that afflict women when they choose men, and she admits the exception!

VI THE MAGIC FLAGSTONE

—in every culture, there are dreams of winning lotteries—

In dreams of innocence
that free all conscience from remorse,
with the Virgin at their side,
my angels slumbered in their cradles,
when, furtively, one calm day,
my heart leaping with joy
I went out alone seeking fortune.

———

I went after a prized treasure,
no one else even knew of,
I was the only one with savvy,
and it wasn't just of silver or gold,
that treasure without peer
was all anyone could want.

———

I was never rich or lucky,
but I saw I could be so;
I was a hair's breadth from changing
from dry thorn into rose.
And like a pure virgin
who for the first time feels the sweetness
of the buzz of love, so I was feeling
that something asleep inside me
was waking, calling me to venture.

———

And so I forgot
the worries that had consumed me
since I was born,
I saw earth and heaven tinted with hope,
and around me, eternal spring.

———

How the sun was shining!
How gently the river murmured!

And the wee bird sang in flight,
    while I walked
    with light step to my goal.

      ——

    Whitening like snow,
    there were clothes and sheets
spreäd on brambles on the mountain,
    oft scattered, oft piled;
just as white clouds dab a serene sky,
lit by sun, they dabbed the landscape
    like no other light.

      ——

    By the inlet on its green shore,
    some win and some lose;
while boys played in the toiling waves,
    the guardian angel passed
    one spot by,
    and though the boy's parents wept
his absence as they buried him,
    the elders said with compassion:
—He's free now of pain.

      ——

    The carts squealed relentlessly,
while the carters chanted slowly
    to their rhythm;
    and here a spring flowed,
as there in the quarry, the metallic echo
of the picks of the stonemasons.
Closer, dogs were barking
and wind stirred in the foliage
from the gulleys to the hills…
¡What peace! ¡What sun!... ¡What bliss!

      ——

    —In the end, Luck, you tire,
and though I hunger for my share, you deny me
    my inheritance of pleasure,

granting me worry and quarrels,
        the very ones you want to,
you gïve me in fistfuls for free.

        —

        This I was saying,
as blissful as could be,
        while I walked
        so happy and sure
of finding the fortune I awaited,
just as I know that, to those who seek, G/d gives.

        —

Couched in boxwoods and weeds
        the magic I craved
called out like a blackbird in its nest,
over the murmur of rolling waters
        at the distant mill…
        I turned back to the pasture,
followed the path through the broom
and finally arrived!... and, on a flagstone
where the crow perches each morning;
        a noble horseman,
jaunty plume in his hatband
and dressed in silk and rhinestones
like a Moorish swashbuckler,
        called to me cunningly,
        so luminously
that he seemed from heaven, not earth.

        —

—It's him! I said in trepidation,
        but he of the magic, skilled
for aeons in dealing with women,
not startled at all to see me,
smiled and called me from afár.

        —

    And the sky was rosy as the sun set,
while in oak woods and gulleys

quiet breezes blew,
      suave and vigorous,
like promises awaited, now fulfilled.

———

      I don't know what I felt
seeing that he kept calling me;
      half worried and half surly,
with baleful courage,
I went toward him, full of desire,
like a moth to a flame.

———

    In his hands, a diamond sceptre,
he tapped on the strange flagstone
that then opened, just as seeds burst
      from ripe pomegranate:
      and with soothing voice
      and like bearing,
—¡Let's go! he said generously, on down!

———

    And I went just as simple leaf falls into calm
current that carries it peacefully
at first in its crystalline waters
to gïve it a loving grave
      on the neighbouring banks,
and then later lifts it, wrenched
      in dark flood,
to the storm-tossed abyss of the sea.

———

    I entered thinking I was in heaven!
Why does evil have such power?
      For how it enchants the eye
and hides its ardent desire,
      never tired or full;
there my eyes went, and were snatched up
as never before, and in love.

———

For hidden treasure
        with its shine and beauty,
who of woman born,
        what mortal creature
would not have been seduced and fooled?

        ——

    And in the light of the half-open door,
without temerity, I was so absorbed,
I stared at the splendid chambers,
one long gallery after another,
and as if I were dead to everything
        apart from from what I saw,
I exclaimed in the supreme height of happiness.

        ——

—Here, Creátor, is the universe's treasure
        without a doubt;
here is that which is imagined but
        never accomplished.
        Never will anyone else find
treasure bigger, more blessed, or more pure!

        ——

    So I blasphemed, without fear or care.
Crazy me, blinded by temptation!
        And the shine I saw
just as I'd always fantasized
gave me full faith in what I sought.

        ——

    Thinking that to my good fortune,
heaven on earth had arrived
and the luck I dreamed of had come true,
without a thought for life or death,
forgetting past and present
        and the future altogether,
I only thought of hiding all that treasure
        somewhere
        unbeknownst to others.

———

I stood equal to the powers that be,
forgetting how human nature
is fallible and childish,
and imagining as ever-gushing spring
     these riches upon riches,
and ostentatious and prideful,
I said as I followed the handsome horseman,
—Given I found you so easily,
so as to best enjoy what's mine, tell me
where to dive in.

———

—Wherever you wish, my lady and queen,
     he answered generously
     in his gracious voice,
whatever here you love is yours,
but first let's drink, you and I,
     from this golden goblet,
to the evils left to us and to those we leave,
and to the good that smiles on us from the dawn
of an April morning that'll never end.

———

—Well let's drink! ¡Drink up!
I repeated, befuddled and not from wine,
without first making the sign of the cross
so that the drink would do me good…
and into the fresh and limpid waters
     let's both go down;
     we'll wet both mouths…

———

I will never forget that moment
when incredible luck turned infernal torment,
     as from inside the goblet
     suddenly arose
one snake's head after another;
unloosed, they darted at me,

and all together
they rose up at once
and into my very side
they sank their venomous stingers.

———

I fell, fell wounded
and almost lifeless,
and still on top of me, they went wild
with their mortal poison
one accursed serpent after another.

———

Greát fog spread
in the South, and into the gulley
the pretty horseman vanished;
and thick cloud swollen with lightning,
looming from shadowy Compostela
visible on the far horizon,
just as cold night's dull line is visible
in the dead of afternoon,
confused my simple mind.

———

And there above the flagstone
where the crow perches each morning,
I found myself without fortune,
bade farewell to sweet illusion,
alone and wretched like no other creature,
poisoned, sad, and badly hurt.

———

And I don't know whose rough voice murmured
in the whistling wind:
—Like you, foul treasure
left here by elves
and awaiting greed,
all magic's earthbound:
for such huge pleasures, huge evil's our return.

—We loathed each other so much,
we wished each other so much ill,
that you died without seeing me,
and since then, I breathe anew.
Now it's my turn
to depart and the priest asks
that I forgïve you, for soon
united we'll be again.
The priest's gone mad!
Us together…! No more, I think;
if you're with the Almighty,
I'll head to the devil.

This a widow old
and stubborn as a ram,
said of her late husband,
alrëady gnawed by worms.
And as she spoke,
she too was dying.
But it's said she and her hubby
found each other again in hell
hand to hand and elbow to elbow
like two long-lost pals.

—How'd you get here?
the widow asked the old guy;
well then, since you've gone to the devil,
I'm going where G/d is.
And without knowing how
she soared to heaven;
but found the door shut
tight by St. Peter.

—¡Knock! ¡knock! open up, it's me!
the old widow croaked.
—¡No way! answered the Apostel,
grabbing the latch.

—But I swore I wouldn't
end up where he is, dear St. Peter...
—No way! the Saint repeated,
retreating inside.
—In the name of your keys,
you sure make a good doorman,
and how you mutter. It's easy to see
you're pleased with yourself!

But I gave my oath, and G/d insists
that we fulfill our vows.
For the third time! Will you open up?
—Not at three nor at three hundred;
the wife goes where her husband is:
To hell, go to hell
with him, forever and evermore!
—Bosh, my Saintly dearest Peter,
how can you pretend to judge
when you've always wandered free,
never were you married
not on earth nor in heaven!
You've had every comfort
you could ask for, you devil!
And you won't accord me even one?
For I too want comfort.
If on earth I walked in chains,
there's no way I want chains now;
at death we part, we spouses,
just as the priests say.
Once we two split up,
me and my husband, it meant
forever! That said,
well I'm just as stubborn as you.
You don't want me in heaven's glory?
Well I swore I'd not go to hell
where he is; that's it,
and there things stand.
Whatcha going to do with me?
Will I go to limbo with unbaptized babies?
I don't care! I'm alreády in it

to the ends of my hair.
—What the haw is up with that woman?
old St. Peter said in anger:
heavens to Betsy...
—Phhh, sir, quit haranguing
and let me in...
—No, no and no. ¡Effin'ell!
Get outa here! And pop, he booted her
straight down to hell.
—But I swóre! I alreády told you...
screamed the widow, I'm not going in.
Lawrdy Lawrd... *sursum corda*;
I'm back, and I'm not budging.

    And she didn't budge, no, didn't budge.
Where? No one really knew,
or knew if it was becaus' G/d heard her
or because the devil didn't want her.
All we know and we know well,
is that she blows on wings of wind
frightening children
in the dark nights of winter,
making lovers jealous,
wrecking weddings,
ruining marriages...
Why didn't St Peter just take her?
For now she walks free and freely
makes our earthly lives a hell.
So cross your fingers, my lasses,
if you hope to have a wedding;
for where she's at, not one man
you'll find to save you.

Another case where the teller blames a woman for all kind of social harms... yet, we have to wonder... *why'd she get rid of him in the first place?*

VIII IN CORNES
—a gorgeous pastoral poem, yet...—

I

Beautiful field in Cornes,
when you dress yourself in lilies,
you dress my soul
in sombre thoughts.
Of Cornes, such a pretty place,
where roads cross from all over:
although covered with roses,
even roses can be blighted.

Amidst the stones, wallflowers;
amidst the görse, bluebells;
between the mosses, violets;
rivulets between the meadows.
Downstream is the millhouse,
Compostela is upstream....
Upstream or downstream,
all is peaceful in the land.

Bells resound from Conxö,
inviting us to meditation,
oxen drink in your river
and sun gladdens after rain.
From your earthly houses
smoke rises and roosters crow...
Who in such a fresh refuge
would admit to sadness' mark!

Where there's folk, there's sorrow;
but in your fields, my land,
I imagine sorrow is most deep
when you seem most glad.
Those trills of birds,
those echoes, hovering
mists and flowers,
in the sad soul, how they weigh!

Wandering in wild grasses
I see an orphan lass
who sadly murmurs:
—My Virgin, if I were a rose!
—Why be a rose, dear child?
I asked her warmly,
and she answers smiling,
—Because roses don't go hungry.

Uphill, up the hill,
we retrace our steps.
We're fleeing this peaceful scene,
this enemy of sadness—
What dark contrast there is
between nature's tranquil
rest, and the harsh worries
that slay the simple spirit!

II

Oh, Cross of Ramírez, you rise stárk
from Agros on the esplanade, between field roses:
the late sun rests its last ray on you
like a golden dream rests on a sad soul.

Sometimes in summer, I sit at your foot
and listen silently, as afternoon ends;
ünder mute stones that hold your secrets,
I imagine the smooth sound of a harp echo,
incomprehensible music that speaks of other worlds.

Just as at dawn from the Colossus of Memnon,
divine sounds are heard, that charm all souls!

III

I hate you, fresh field,
with your green walls,
with your high laurels
and your pale paths
seeded with violets,
shaded by arbours.
    I hate you, headlands smoothed
and lit by setting sun,
where on serene nights
I've seen the moon blaze,
and where in better days
I wandered in the hills.
    And you too, little
river, more beautiful than any,
how dreary you too are
as I muse in memory...
It's because I loved you all so much,
that I hate you now so deeply!

"...the narrative web is a thin film constantly threatened with bursting.
For, when narrated identity is unbearable, when the boundary between
subject and object is shaken, and when even the limit between inside
and outside becomes uncertain, the narrative is what is challenged
first. [...] At a later stage, the unbearable identity of the narrator and of
the surroundings that are supposed to sustain her can no longer be
narrated but *cries out* or is *descried* with maximal stylistic intensity
(language of violence, of obscenity, or of a rhetoric that relates the text
to poetry)." Kristeva, *PoH*, 141

I

Watching in our fields how
once again they're tying back roses
I said: —Where on earth, dear G/d,
will I go to hide now!
And thought of San Lourenzo
amid silent oakwoods.

———

Back then those old oak trees,
their roots emerging,
their rounded canopies bald,
and already clothed with mosses,
they spoke to careworn and lonely
souls, of all that's sad.

———

The cypress that looms ahead
behind the convent wall,
and the slim belltower
grass-draped and mossy,
from the pasture, it and the roadside cross
were both mute sentinels.

———

And the Christ who in the stone arch
bows his weary head,
lonely, as if still on Golgotha
wrestling the agonies,
fills oppressed hearts
with resignation.

———

And were I to penetrate the cloisters,
        deserted and in ruins,
        never would the world see
        a clearer image of oblivion,
        or would a greáter silence
        on earth surround me.

        ——

In the crannies of the hidden spring
        digitalis grew freely
        between wild violas,
        amid boxwood trees.
        ¡How pleased death would've been
        in that deserted place!

        ——

That's why, on watching in the fields
        as they tie the roses back again,
        I said: —Where on earth, dear Gwd,
        will I go to hide now?
        And toward the woods of San Lourenzo
        I walk in silence.

        II

Where'd my blessed refuge gone?
        I heard strange sounds.
        Stonemasons came and went
        through those secluded woods.
        It was as if a pious hand
        cared for the destitute!

        ——

In a glance I sized up all inside...
        all was gleaming,
        every stone a mirror,
        and the old convent, a palace
        shawled with pretty flowers.
        How disheartening!

Dark clouds fast shadowed
     my astonished eyes:
     and wearier than ever,
     I fled… ! For my beloved refuge
that had seemed a monk's clean soul,
was now sunk in worldly grime.

March, 1880

In the restoration of San Lourenzo, Rosalía sees a symbol of conflictive historical change, in which capitalism devours all of cultural value in the name of modernity and creates simulacrae in their place: a Disney Worlding of history (Baudrillard, but Rosalía said it first) that unlinks cultures from space and time and local life. Is this where being "earthbound" gets us? With no base but information, signs. Yet the date is sure. It is the only dated poem in the entire volume. *And Lourenzo? Ironically (or not, if you read Derrida's* Mal d'archive) *he is the patron saint of archivists...*

Leafless
Twice Widowed
Living and Dead

HAVANA-BOUND![14]

I

His oxen sold,
his cows sold off,
the soup pot gone
and no blankets on his bed.
    His cart in hock
and his fields too;
now he owns only
the shirt he wears.
    —Maria, I'm young,
I don't want to beg;
I'll head off somewhere
to try to make good.
    Galicia is poor,
so I'm Havana-bound...
¡Farewell, farewell, treasure
of my heart!

II

When no one's looking,
their faces cloud over; glum,
they shift like shadows
over plains and fields.
    One, on a headland
sits brooding and wistful;
another leans on an oak,
eyes raised to the infinite.
    One, poised at the fountain,
is intent on the murmur

---

[14] A common destination of late 19th century Galician immigrants (when ¼ of Galician men emigrated). Probably, says Angueira, the first Galician poem on transatlantic emigration (earlier emigration was to Castile, as in the poem with the singing workers with their scythes).

of falling water, and mutely exhales
the saddest of sighs.
    They're losing their homeland...!
Forced sacrifice, supreme.
Poverty all dark around them,
oh, and ahead lies an abyss...

                III

    The sea harshly flails whoever suffers,
and against banks of fog
break irritated waves
of Cantabrian brine.
    Gulls shriek
far out there.... ¡So far!...
from quiet and solitary shores
that invite relaxation and love.
    The compact queue of human beings
gleams sunlit as it moves and turns;
nearer and more slowly, it curves
along Parrote's ancient city walls.
    Worry clenches the heart;
laughter rises, swearing's heard,
and blasphemies mix with sighs.
Where are these men bound?
    In a month, in the broad cemetery
of Havana, or in its woods,
go and see what they became.
They sleep forever forgotten!
Poor mothers who raised them,
and poor lasses who lovingly await their return!

                IV

    ¡Onward, my mates!
Earth exists for men.
They who only see in front of their noses,
ignorance will eat them.

¡Adiante! Gwd helps those who get moving!
And though we'll be far from Galicia,
you'll see when we return
¡that the oaks keep growing!
Tomorrow's the day we're to sea, friends!
Tomorrow, in the hands of G/d!
    Joy's in our features,
in our hearts, fierce striving,
and the harmonious ring of hope's bell,
distant, a death knell!

                    V

    This man went, that guy's gone,
and all, all of them leave.
Galicia, void of men
who can work your soil.
You have orphans instead,
and lonely fields;
and childless mothers
and fatherless bairns.
And you have hearts that endure
absence all their lives,
twice-widowed, grief living, grief dead;
inconsolable!

‖ NEVER MIND THE DEAD!

I

We'll profane the shade of the woods!
   And before these mute witnesses—
   river, springs, and heavens—
   I swear I'll sever my old ties!
The hours from the past that leapt
   across untold abysses,
   won't return… ¡never mind!
   We can't be martyrs to memory.

II

There's a nest of wild roses
   near the hidden spring,
   and a clover meadow
   carpets the shade all around.
For awhile now, breezes stir,
   in the leaves, goldfinches sing,
   the daisies smile upon me,
   and I hear the river's murmur.

III

Without love, this life is dark
   and the sun has lost its shine.
   Let my last sip of all
   be of a celestial wine.
It's said that forgetting's a wide bed
   for the destitute sleeper;
   let's both of us imbibe together
   in these woods among the thorns.

IV

How harmoniously the rough drone
    of pines resounds in the heights!
    I imagine pines watch us
    serenely from such peaks.
And I seem to glimpse in the mist,
    in the vagaries of the infinite,
    the sad and blurred profile
    of my lost reveries,
and the shades clumsily dráw near me
    through these hills and crannies,
    shades of my beloved dead
    and of my living pain.
¡But I don't care! From the ancient pasture
    we'll profane these sanctuaries...
    Sit at my side and tell me,
    tell me... what so many've heard.

V

You stand fierce and slender and your eyes
in mine are steady as stars
    sleeping; they say that love's
    divine touch rests in the eyes.
I look at you serenely,
    my gaze is of cold pebbles
    as I count the turbulent beats
    of your heart.
The atmosphere thickens round us.
    Every day it's the same!
    As birds each have their song
    you, heart, have your rhythm.
But tears inundate my face,
    and deep into my soul
    slow disgust penetrates
    its double-edged blade.
¡Ho! Stand back from me; I can't
    profane this place of refuge,

for my heart though crazy
can't murder its own self.
Rest easy, all my angered shades,
for I am dead to those who are alive.
Sacred you've remained, oh woods!
And you, my spirit, are unsullied![15]

---

[15]Could it be? Yes, it could! The woman whose husband has long emigrated felt desire for another on a walk in the woods. Almost. Unsullied!!

‖ OUR HOME AND NATIVE LAND!

I

Under the placid shade of our good
         country chestnuts;
under leafy oakwoods
         that make living sweet;
near the fig tree, at my father's house,
         so old no one can count its years,
what happy tales, what loving
         words are spoken there!
Laughter heard in the peaceful evenings
         of loving April!
And there too, such sad farewells
         we've so often heard!

II

—To have a house, is alreády to have half a life.
         A few tiles for a roof,
four logs to burn in our hearth,
         and endless work!
Courage, courage! And the hope, wretched,
         that while you still have
a few sad walls here, as bare
         and sad as you inherited them,
no one can dispossess you.
         ¿No one? Oh yes, poverty can.

III

Oven without bread, hearth without wood,
         no cricket sings there,
and if it weren't for the aches that gnaw him,
         the wretch'd be alone in his suffering.
Without food or coat he shivers,
         because the subtle winds

whistle dank between the stones
        and make all the doors sigh.
What else can be done, Lord, if destitution
        is all around him?
Leave the land that bore him and the house
        in which he hopes to die?
No, no, for winter's done and magnificent
        spring will come.
Alreády the trees bud in his garden.
        Alreády April's at the door!
And even though at sad times, there's torrential rain,
        at others, the sun laughs;
already the soil can be sown; the hunger
        of the poor will flee.
Oh! those born in you, beautiful Galicia,
        want to die in you.

        IV

¡Oh, my vines of Albariño grapes,
        gïve me shade!
¡Oh you, white flowering elder,
        you cure all illness!
¡Oh, you, all told, my garden so beloved
        and my fields of greens!
¡I will not leave you, and will banish
        my worries, somehow!
Summer comes to fill all with its fruits,
        all are now rich,
the birds have grain out in the fields,
        and shelter in foliage.
Nights are peaceful and serene,
        the moonlight always clear,
between the rooftiles its rays enter
        and fall on my bed,
and I sleep lit by its lamp
        that gïves light to poor folk:
beautiful lamp, eternally beautiful,
        consolation of mortals.

V

These many mountain paths
        drop into deepest valleys...
There above, the whoosh whoosh of wild pines;
        below, sweet peace.
On the peak, clear light, purest air,
        wild solitude,
mysterious sounds that awaken
        thoughts of fierce freedom.
Penetrating perfumes provoke crazy
        strange desires;
belów, in loving calm, the caress of
        breezes stirs
amid the leaves, carrying tales from town
        in their wings,
echoes of some fresh and sonorous voice
        virginal in timbre.
The clamour of the village churchbell's
        prolonged ring,
the rough thunder of the mill dam,
        and the rhythmic thump
as the washerwoman beats white linen
        against a stone.

VI

   ¡Yes, yes! God made this enchanting land
        to be lived in and enjoyed;
a paradise in miniature, copy
        of what Adam lost.
This placid sun that gives us light;
        these breezes from the sea;
this clement air; these tiny fields
        found only here;
the cherished language that is ours,
        such sweet solace,
that it only speaks in utter affection.
        This land touches every heart;

of that there's no doubt…, the Maker made it
        to be loved and to love.
Oh, Galicia, that sleeps the dreams of angels,
        and on waking weeps
tears that, though they console the aches,
        cannot cure its ills!

        VII

How your children love you; how it eats them
        to leave your soil behind;
they sigh inconsolably if they must head
        away to live in other lands.
Though their bodies be in distant regions
        their spirit's always here,
for they live and breathe the memories
        of their homeland.
And they live the hope, the ardent hope
        of being in Galicia again…
And, how can they not adore you so,
        blessed and beloved mother,
how can they not hope not to die far from your breast
        that offers the honey of all honey,
and is glory and joy and paradise
        in this earthly world!

        VIII

How beautifully you were made, beloved homeland,
        unlucky beauty!
What tender and melancholy serenity
        I feel when I contemplate you!
Oh why, oh why between flowers must thorns
        be twisted
into the crown that marks your brow
        with evergreen?
¡Oh Galicia! ¡Galicia! the sonorous harp
        will soon breák free
of the dry branch where it hangs forgotten

and has slept for centuries.
The bards, your children, will lift their voices
to the rhythm of its chords
and fill the world with lofty harmonies
simply to laud you.

Without a song the day would never end
Without a song the road would never bend
When things go wrong a man ain't got a friend
That field of corn would never see a plow
That field of corn would be deserted now
A man is born but he's no good no how
I got my trouble and woe but, sure as I know, the Jordan will roll
And I'll get along as long as a song, strong in my soul
I'll never know what makes the rain to fall
I'll never know what makes that grass so tall
I only know there ain't no love at all
I've-a got...

1929, music by Vincent Youmans, lyrics by Billy Rose and Edward Eliscu (in public domain in Canada since 1999)

    I wove my cloth alone,
alone my turnip field I seeded,
alone I fetch wood on the mountain,
alone I watch it glowing in the hearth.
Not at fountain nor at pasture,
when I was dying from my load
did he come to help me lift it
nor will he help me set it down.
¡Sorrow! The wind whistles,
the cicada trills to its beat...;
the cauldron simmers... but, oh, my soup
we two will dine alone.
Shush, turtledove, your cooing
makes me want to die:
shush, cicada, for when you trill,
I feel bleak yearnings.
My beloved man is lost
no one knows where he is...
Swallow who crossed
the waves of the sea with him:
swallow, fly, fly,
come and tell me where he is.

Springs run dry,
oaks drop their leaves;
yet your soul inhabits springtime:
sees out there but dawn.

———

And for all you hear of the world,
for all you hear of life...
Your thirst won't be quenched by what others drank
from cursèd waters.

———

But when your evening comes,
and your autumn has its time,
come tarry slowly at my tomb,
and lay your remorse with mine.

Dreaming the return of the emigrant...

VI FEELING NO ONE'S PAIN BUT MINE

Some hurt in wishing to console,
others stick their finger in the wound;
but worst of all is the traitor
with his crooning: —It'll get better soon!

——

Then, with peaceful conscience,
he goes off, happy as a lark,
leaving us in pain that, if it doesn't kill us,
makes our life so stark.

——

And, as so often happens,
when he who hurts is hurt in turn,
he'll claim his pain will outlast eternity,
and fill heaven with his howling moan.

—Just as meat's sold in the market,
        that rotter's sold you out!
—But what does it matter that he sold me out,
        I can't forget him!
—He near killed you, merciless, and left you,
        that turncoat left you.
—I'll die a sad and forgotten woman,
        but forget him… ¡no!
—Like one walks on grass, he walked on you…
        He despised you, and you won't detest him?
—Though he hate me, and walk on me, and curse me,
        I must forgïve him.
—You're so unwavering, you crazy lass,
        you and your loyalty!
But, even if you pardon him, G/d, who's just,
        won't let him go free.

        (An incredulous bloke, nearby,
grins a devilish grin)
—Trust in God and don't go so fast.
        ¡God! Who knows if there's one?
(An old biddy passing by) —Whoever screws up
will pay, I know, sooner or later.
        (Another guy)—We wander in the dark,
blind to where we're headed.
But grab what you can while it's there to grab,
better to nab than keep on waiting.
        (A roisterer) —There's as many men
as there are thoughts and intentions.
But rare indeed is one who in dying
can forgive the one who killt him.

A dialogue, overheard, ends in a marketplace of voices…

VIII

It was a bone dry Easter, then
rained on the Baptist's Day in June;
to Galicia now a famine
is coming close and soon.
    Filled with melancholy,
they gaze at the sea with dread;
they who to other countries
now must go to earn their bread.

IX

I will not tend the roses
I have of him, nor tend his doves;
they can just wither, as I wither,
they can just die, as I am dying.

we are here back to thoughts...
for it is thoughts that have us dying...

I bear an ache
inside my heart;
I bear it, and no one
knows why I do.
Lush banks
of the serene Miño,
where tiny birds
find their mirror,
and sheep graze
amid daisies,
only you know
how I feel.
    Close to a cliff
from where a creek springs,
in the shade of a pine
hüge and gentle
that proudly howls
when moved by wind,
my secret sleeps
as if in the grave.
But though it sleeps there
it lives awake in me.
    I bear an ache
inside my heart;
so greát, greater
than, good God, I'd prayed for.
What I would gïve, banks
of the serene Miño,
to be one of those fallow hills
harboured at your side.
Without fears or ache,
in summer or in winter,
one century after another,
they live where I wish to,
with grassy fields for manor,
and spacious sky as roof.

to be a hill, to be a field, to be one with the natural world…

My thoughts, how crazily you fly!...
    Where are you headed?
¿Where? ¿Where? If I can't tell,
    no one else will know.

———

From the spring to the river,
    from the fields down to the sea.
What do you seek, you crazies? If I can't tell,
    no one else will know.

———

My thoughts... why do you always
    torment me?
Why are you with me daily, if where you head
    no one else will know?

———

Like a moth, you seek the flame
    that will burn you up...
and of the sad death you'll come to,
    no one else will know.

The inability—felt by many, esp. women—to speak to others of struggles resulting from betrayal, assault, boundaries disrespected— is often linked to depression (woe). The life toll is greater than one imagines. *#metoo*

You up and left one day,
you, the one I loved;
you fled the land
that held such joy
and such delight.
You said: —Maria,
sweeter than honey,
prettier than flowers,
my dove unsurpassed,
don't cry, don't cry,
may absence enliven
not kill; don't forget
the sweet love
we were lucky to share.
¡I'm gone! But if right now
luck's betrayal
brings us grief,
never will I forget you,
so greatly I adored you
so greatly I loved you.
¡Farewell, my life!
I'll always hold you
in my heart, though
I won't see you again.
Await me, for I do avow
by Manitou most holy,
that if I don't die,
here I'll return.
Die, you did not die,
and though I waited...
how well you knew
what you were saying,
of love that you *had*!
The years passed,
flowers withered;
black hair
gone white;

and nevermore, never...
for a wish has great power!
...did you wish to return:
I've lived to see it.

The "mutations in the tissue of the sensible" (Rancière) that Rosalía provokes, in writing in Galician. Changes in the tissue of what can be said change our perception of art, by entering into something that was not art, making it artful. And now art is new...

The next poem recounts a similar tale, but is written in the man's voice, reporting a dialogue—we receive the woman's voice via the man...

    —You're báck, Rosa of Anido?
Who knew I'd see you so soon!
And all the witches with you, Rosa,
there in the town they tarry,
and you look hálf-dead
and wild-eyed, and your voice cracks.
    —It's just I ache, and from afar,
bit by bit, I've come back dying;
but… you'll see me flush again,
for now I see you, I feel alive.
    —Crazy Rosa, what's with you!
Do you still recall those days?
    —I still remember! How could I forget,
when they're all I think of.
We drank together at that fountain,
together we rested on that gate,
we gathered hay together in the meadow,
and we went together to take the air
in August when the moon
rose pale over the hills.
These memories consumed me,
away from you and far from home…
But you, tell me, didn't you remember
and don't you remember it all?
    —You ask me, lass, when
I've a memory like a sieve!
And moreover, Rosa, I'll tell you all
so that you banish such thoughts.
I drank with other girls from that fountain,
rested with others on that gate,
and with so many in the August moonlight
did I go to take the air!
Don't you agree, sweets, that a man
weighed down by memories
has to cast them off,
or they'd only trouble his thinking.
I loved you once, Rosa, I did love you;

but as the song goes, love and wind
when they've done their doing,
flee, lass, fast as they had come.
And what are we to do, Rosa,
if that's the way things are?
¡Farewell! To Havana I embark on Sunday;
and though you cry now, don't fear,
it's heartache, not death's wake,
and, all said and done, time heals.

XIV

I want to leave, to leave.
Where to, I do not know.
Fog blinds my eyes.
How can I find my path?

———

In such a restlessness
that won't let me live:
I crave and don't know what I crave,
it all seems the same to me.

———

I want to leave, to leave,
say some on the brink of death;
oh, they want to flee death,
and death goes with them!

    My purest perfume
I'd gïve you were I a rose,
my most serene murmur
if a wave of sea.
The most loving kíss
were I a ray of dawn,
if G/d... But I alreády know you
want nothing of me, not even glory.

a call to the absent emigrant who no longer sends news...

    —Doctor, her head hurts...
Surgeon, her hand is aching...
But if it's the spirit that pains her,
what medicine can you gïve?
    —For sickness of the soul
there's no earthly cure:
pray to the Maker to take her from you;
maybe in heaven she'll heal.

—Though you serve me Ribeiro wine of Avia,[16]
and all other liqueurs and every dish
on which kings feast and that the world offers,
my dear mother, something's missing.
    Though you hold me in your hands like an icon
and though you clothe me all in finery
and usher me to the Court of Spain,
my dear mother, something's missing.
    And though you give me gold, and silver,
diamonds and dark pearls, white pearls and emeralds
all there are in the world, you give me nothing,
for, sweet mother, something's missing.
My wings are clipped of beautiful hopes,
and there's no joy where hope's missing.

---

[16]Ribeiro da Avia=Ribadavia, a town with a Sephardic history, home each July to the *Mostra internacional de teatro de Ribadavia*, Galicia's most important theatre festival, 35 years old in 2019.

From here I see the camiño
and who knows where it goes;
and since I don't know,
I want to go and walk it.
Narrow it winds
between meadows and green rows
and at times it's clear, at times hidden,
glinting further on.
But always, always tempting me
with its pretty clarity,
so that I think, I don't know why,
of the towns where it passes,
of the oakwoods that shadow it,
of the springs that will water it.
Camiño, white path,
I don't know where you go;
but everytime I see you,
I want to go and walk you.
You head to Santiago,
you head to O Portal,
in San Andrés you tarry,
you arrive at San Cibrán,
and in the end, you vanish... who knows
where? How you lure me!
Would that I could vanish on you
and never find myself again...
But you keep going, keep going,
always headed where you do,
always toward where you're going,
and I stay stuck where
my misfortune's rooted.
I don't flee, no, for even if I fled
from one place to another,
from myself no one, no one,
no one will free me.

The doves were kíssing,
sweet swallows flew,
wind played with the grasses
pocked with daisies,
and the washerwomen sang
as the rivulet ran.
    One after another they all left,
and there she remained alone,
her sad head bowed
near a shady arcade...
    Then who knows what shades,
perhaps of vivid memories,
perhaps of long-gone monks,
passing mystic in procession,
she saw, in those fallow fields
that she both loved and feared.
    She trembled in ache and anguish,
and with a bitter smile,
gazing at bare jasmine
that would soon burst into leaf,
she murmured, her eyes
tearful:
    —All returns, all turns again,
except the thing for which I yearn;
everything, everything here remains:
I alone try to flee.
I'll no longer see you, flowers,
adorning these cornices;
nor hear your murmurs,
fountain that invites pleasure,
nor contemplate you, stones,
witnesses of my heartache.
Others will come to profane you,
while I die forgotten.
    Footsteps rang out under the domes,
a strong breeze did blow,
there was heard a cáckle

as if it came from hell;
it was the goblin of the cloister
who, mindful of the past,
was laughing at bleak worries
and at the abandoned lass.

    How her heárt weighs,
oh how much it aches in her!
Neither day nor night
bring halt to her sorrow.
Arbiter, look what you've wrought;
¡Arpenteur, cure her!
    And her broken heart,
too, how it hurts her!
All I know well's that there's
no cure for heartache.
Seigneur, let her go to her rest
in the earth that raised her;
may dust turn to dust,
and the spirit turn toward heaven, dear G/d.

The sun come to warm me
gave me shivers,
as if a savage North blast
swept me viciously away.
I heard a bagpipe
happy-sounding,
and it gave me
goosebumps;
and I trembled like grass
on the river bank
does when touched by
the current.
My aching soul,
oh my body so simple,
the bagpipe wounds you,
sunlight chills you..
My soul, my body,
if it's not a curse,
it's that death wants me
for its garden row.

XXII

   Always you await death,
but death never comes,
poor wretch! Do you think sorrow
kills quickly?
Never, it's like tuberculosis;
after gnawing and gnawing
it leaves a body only when
there's nothing left.
          When the waters of sorrow
pour into the cup without stopping,
          death is the one remedy
          that will cure life.

—I'm heading home;
what'll I tell your wife Antona?
—Well, so as not to spark a war,
and so they don't cross the sea to lynch me,
forget you even saw me.
As for the rest... you're free as an ox...
You aleády know the sayings, pal:
freedom first,
and have your cake and eat it too.
    —Better to be bachelor on this shore, as they say,
than married over there with children
and stuck sweating in the corn...
I get it, pal!
    —As far as Antona and her doings go,
and even though I miss her
as over here I neither know nor hear...
Whoever knows and sees nothing... always forgïves.
When I get old,
I'll haul my bones back to the village,
as I have to bring something home to our beloved land;
but while I'm still young, I can't do it,
and speaking of wives,
over there I've got Antona, here Rosa.
    —That one's mother of the year,
my good man Antón of Riaño,
but I'll tell you frankly
that all women are the devil,
and even if that's how it is,
between ours and another's
more or less pleasing,
well...., woman for woman, ours is the best.
    —Ours is the one we love and who loves us,
for when caring is lacking,
you think you've a dove in the nest
and it's really a cobra, daughter of demons.
    —If the cobra's head is split,
it pays with its life.

But take Antona's patience
how will you repay it, in good conscience?
Who'll cure the deep wound of her sorrow?
    —Cut that crap of conscience and sorrow,
they have no place
in talk of women and love.
It's up to her to gët over it if she wants to;
and tell her that when I have it,
I'll gïve her something to get over it with.
¡And now, farewell, until we meet again!

here Rosalía enacts
a poetic inference and shift, an interlock at different angles...

I have a nest of crazy thoughts
hidden near the hearth,
and as soon as night comes
and the fire's lit
and I hang the pot and sit to spin
in my favourite spot,
while the soup heats, then I call them:
—¡Come, my pretties!
     And they run and clamber
all happy to have me to themselves,
to be with their mother, their lady,
their sole affection.
And how we whisper among ourselves
always of him, ¡oh my G/d!
Of him, who's gone…, and left me
with an aching heart.
     How many sorrows, how many
deep sighs of lament
have tormented me! How many,
right from my heart!
But all in secret,
for we speak of it to no one;
it's unthinkable that I should murmur
of what he's done to me.
     Talk of you to just anybody…me?
Never, my sweetheart;
you are my husband and I your wife, and I must
hush my grief at your straying.
I confide only in my own crazed thoughts,
for they are my friends
and so discreet, so much so
that they say only what I allow.
     Without them, my Joe, what'd become of me?
Alone here, when once I was with you;

---

[17] this poem is the twin of the preceding poem, from a woman's viewpoint!

bursting with sorrow, as thorns
burst in the fire!
    Many times, yes, many…,
to keep me awake, those rotten thoughts!
they come into my bed,
and where you slept, they nestle;
but I, as I do now,
so as not to cry a river,
so as not to get up at dawn
with eyes red as burning embers
when I go to market,
I know to call them despicable.
Stop tormenting me and go hide
in your little burrow!
And I bid them farewell in passing
with a loving kíss…
But though I kíss them, the kíss
is for you alone, dear Joe.
    Come back, back to me, for though I claim
I can live consoled
by my crazed thoughts, perhaps,
perhaps they're leading me to death, ¡oh my God!
    Joe, Joe, born of a woman
and with children from another,
¡oh! as your father'd have died without your mother,
I'm dying without you, dear Joe.

Hush, black dog, don't howl
at the door of the one I cherish;
crows, don't fly across
the roof where he lies ill.
You who glimmer, you wandering souls,
just scram, don't make him fear.
If it's that you wish someone to die,
I know of one robust and happy,
go rob *him* of his life
and take *him* with you to hell.

XXVI WESTERN TOWERS[18]

The river courses
on its way,
and I went to it
near Laíño,
weak with sorrows
that abide in me.

———

Thus burdened,
where was I going?
The Virgin might know
what I don't know;
but perhaps it was myself
I was fleeing.

———

Amidst hayfields,
deep and shady,
like a serpent
with burnished scales,
it glinted in my eyes
making me greedy.

———

I was so alone!
Not a boat or launch,
nor sail nor oars
brightened the view,
and the meadows too
were all alone.

———

How lovely were
the roses once

———————————————

[18] 9th century fortress at the mouth of the River Ulla, facing the sea.

that in those fields
bloomed and ¡dropped petals!
But then they withered,
every one.

———

    And sun, like moon
on a night of mist,
glowed trembling
between basket-willows,
pallid
as wax.

———

    Dark and tossed,
the waves lashed out
and in the black density
of the depths,
long wet seaweed's seen
making its furrows there.

———

    Suddenly one thing and another
make me afraid,
and I saw the struggle
of crosses
that loom along the shore
as if in a cemetery.

———

    My love, where are you?
I asked in tears.
Now you've died,
what in the world will I do,
like you, ¡oh towers!,
alone without harbour?

———

    Loneliness consumes me,
tears feed me,

shadows accompany me,
sadness devours me.
Who can live with such
greát grief?

———

    And I know not what dark
damned temptation
froze my spirit,
clouded my sight,
and smiled on me as
only the devil could.

———

    From the deep banks
I looked around…
Rising tides
lapped at the towers,
orphans in the liquid
sheet that engulfed them.

———

    —¡I'm going there! I told them.
—Gïve me sweet death,
waters where sadness
sleeps forever…
I leapt, and the deep
current carried me away.

………………………………..
………………………………..
………………………………..

    Oh, Western Towers!
Tempting evils,
leaden waters
of traitorous calm;
stripped headlands
where the crow rests.

———

Oh, Western Towers!
So solitary and mute,
here you witnessed
my sorrow.
No one sorrowful draws
close to you ever.

———

To the abandoned
you pay your homage,
and even air
does not well up
near you, as if it feared
to bid you farewell.

———

It's the women
whom your sadness touches,
those whose hearts are heavy,
daunted women,
whose struggling souls
are on the path to hell.

———

And if I'm still alive,
it's because a mariner
pulled me from the waves
by my hair,
half moribund,
into the world in which I yearn.

———

Don't ever go,
is my advice,
to the Western Towers,
with a heavy heart.

      —¡Hark! it's bailyffes
      bearing down on the village;
but how to pay taxes, how? if one can't
      even pay the rent!

      ——

They seize everything, for they
have no conscience or soul.
      We'll be out the door,
      children of my womb!

      ——

      May foul death fell you
      before you set foot here!
      The hearts of the poor, on
hearing you, beat so sadly!

      ——

      —Maria, if there weren't
a Maker who rewards and punishes,
      I'd slay those men
like a fox does a hen.

      ——

    —¡Hush! Don't blaspheme,
    for this is a vale of tears…!
¿But why do some have to suffer so much,
and others live their days in plenty?

She's dying of yearning
in town, pining for the village;
the walls of houses spooked her,
as did towers and churches.

———

The cobbled streets seemed to her
grey and stale,
a cemetery where the dead
wandered outside their sad graves.

———

And food tasted to her
of flour without salt and of sour radish,
and she had so few meals,
instead of giving energy, they made her frail.

———

At times, and who knows if in reality
or dream, scents of country fields
reached her from
far riverbanks and pinewoods.

———

She'd go sit then upon a rise,
contemplate the broad horizon,
and, breaking into sighs that drowned her,
in hoarse sobs she'd exclaim: —I'm going!

———

And off she sped without a second thought! Along
with the mortal sorrow that consumed her!
Poor Rosa went off...
but...but... to the next life!

    —Oh, Rosa, take heart,
life brings great aches
to those who live with gusto,
and forgotten will be she who was beloved.
What happened to you, happens to us all
one way or another.
    Don't you remember that lass?
All in her was charm and beauty,
all innocence so pure;
and with deep tenderness
and with a love that could soften stone,
I always called her
my peerless dove, and fount of caring.
It was as if the dove nursed at her breast,
which was so white, it glowed!
And perfume, colour, savour, and I fully
relished Angela's every flavour,
though I didn't even dare to breathe her scent.
Everything about her was dear to me!
    That was long ago, a happy time
and my heart still cherishes its memory,
for after that
and with both of us living apart,
she gone to Ferrol and I to Cambados,
we'd try to meet at the Campelo Fair,
and I sought in her face what you seek in his,
and in her whole being,
that charm which once enchanted me,
I couldn't feel it any more.
    Yet she was the same, tall and pretty,
fresh and flushed,
sweet as honey from the hive;
but to all her spells
I was immune,
and I sought in vain from the past
a changing phantasm that fled
free of love and free of chains.

I meditated a moment,
and with certain remorse and feeling,
I finally realized, my dear Rosa,
that whatever charms I'd fallen for,
they were nothing to me
and that my love had lent her
other charms than those she really had.

For wisdom is not enough,
nor generosity, beauty, nor innocence,
purity, nor virtue:
to be well loved and to love well,
being suffices on its own.

While love abides,
even if you're plain, there's no woman like you,
none more amiable or better looking;
even if you seem horrible and lost, you'd be blessed
among those who are without trying to be;
even if you're a foolish bore, it's that
you have a hidden essence blessed with grace
inside a mysterious reliquary
where only the blind and visionary lover
finds the essence or elixir of life.

But when love flies away, my dearest,
when its blindfold falls,
we have to let love go,
for there's no virtue or power that can hold it,
and the ones who once saw us through a cloud
or transparent bubble,
once the bubble bursts and the cloud passes,
Rosa, Rosa, Rosa, it's gone, it's gone,
it's best they do not look on us.

xxx BURDEN OF SORROW

    So many wildflowers in the valleys,
such festivities and lace
spring from moss and green;
what colours, what foliage in the trees
while breezes gently flit
like the breath of ángels!
    In the meadow reigns a placid calm,
the light falls on the creeks in flashes,
and headlands and ravine deftly
sculpt the landscape,
lightly cloaked in mists
of mysterious afternoon.
    All that's heard is the chirp of birdlets,
the murmuring of waters,
and on the mountaintop, the sad song
of a woman walking,
while the gentle creek accompanies her
in rhythmic monotone murmur.
What sadness so sweet!
What solitude so peaceful!
But for a soul utterly orphaned,
¡what solitude so empty and bitter!

                        ——

        She gazes without looking
        into distant mists,
        vaporous and light
        as the sun paints them red,
        and with hands clasped, and eyes
        raked by tears,
she murmurs sobbing: —I want to go,
for I'm dying here disconsolate…
        Rather than here amid roses,
oh, I want to go to die where he has gone.
        And in the ship's hold
        alone, abandoned,
in love and toward death, to America
to die of grief, she heads out to sea.

In the last three poems of this "book outside the book" that ends *In Leaf,* the widow of living grief either m
forget, go in search of the emigrant, or ...await the return (which brings domestic labour, R reminds us, not re

221

Both far from home
we wander and suffer, that's sure!
But you in your loneliness remember home
and I, remember home—and you.
Both of us wander the world
and our strength gradually dwindles.
But ¡oh! you find your rest when you reach home,
and I'll find mine only in death.

READINGS & HISTORIES (grey = refs edited out in 2016, +=new refs, *=key)

Álvarez, R., et al. *Rosalía de Castro no século XXI: Unha nova ollada*. Santiago: Concello da Cultura Galega, 2014.

*Angueira, Anxo. 'Estudo Introdutorio' in *Follas Novas* by Rosalía de Castro, ed. Anxo Angueira. Vigo: Xerais, 2016 (7-99).

*_____. 'Fixación, Notas, e Comentarios' in *Follas Novas* by Rosalía de Castro, ed. Anxo Angueira. Vigo: Xerais, 2016 (347-467).

Butler, Judith. *Gender Trouble: Feminism and Subversion of Identity*. NY: Routledge, 1990.

_____. *Bodies That Matter*. NY: Routledge, 1993.

_____. *Excitable Speech: A Politics of the Performative*. NY: Routledge, 1997.

_____.*Giving An Account of Oneself*. NY: Fordham U Press, 2005.

+Castro, Olga. "La traducción como mecanismo de (re)canonización: el discurso nacional y feminista de Rosalía de Castro en sus traducciones al inglés," Quaderns. Revista de Traducció 19, 2012, 199-217.

*Derrida, Jacques. *L'écriture et la différence*. Paris: Seuil, 1967 and *Mal d'archive*. Galilée: 1995.

*_____. 'Signature, Event, Context' in *Limited Inc*. Trans. by S. Samuel Weber and Jeffrey Mehlman. Evanston, Il: Northwestern U Press, 1988 (17 and others).

_____. 'Remarks on Deconstruction and Pragmatism,' in *Deconstruction and Pragmatism*. ed. Chantal Mouffe. London: Routledge, 1996 (77-88).

do Cebreiro, María. *Fogar impronunciable. Poesía e pantasma*. Vigo: Galaxia, 2011.

Glissant, Edouard. *La Cohée du Lamentin : Poétique V*. Paris: Gallimard, 2005.

Goldstein, Steve. 'Food-stamp cut, bad weather blamed by Wal-Mart for profit warning,' *MarketWatch*, 13 January 2014. Web. 21 May 2016.

González Fernández, Helena and María do Cebreiro Rábade Villar (eds.) *Canon y subversión. La obra narrativa de Rosalía de Castro*. Barcelona: Icaria, 2012.

+Kristeva, Julia. *Powers of Horror*. Trans. Leon Roudiez. NY: Columbia U Press, 1982.

*Miguélez-Carballeira, Helena. *Galicia, a Sentimental Nation: Gender, Culture and Politics*, Cardiff: U Wales Press, 2013.

_____. 'Rosalía de Castro: Life, Text and Afterlife' in *The Companion to Galician Culture*, ed. Helena Miguélez-Carballeira. London: Tamesis, 2014 (175-191).

Mouffe, Chantal. *The Democratic Paradox*. NY: Verso, 2000 (12, 21).

Moure, Erín. 'Stakes, Poetry, Today,' *My Beloved Wager*. Edmonton: NeWest, 2009 (208).

Nash, Elizabeth. 'Manuel Rivas: Spirits of the Sea,' *The Independent (UK)*, 31 January 2003. Web. 22 May 2016.

Ngai, Sianne. *Ugly Feelings*. Cambridge, MA: Harvard U Press, 2005.

Picchi, Aimee. 'How low-wage employers cost taxpayers $153B a year,' *CBS MoneyWatch*, 13 April 2016. Web. 21 May 2016.

*Rancière, Jacques. *Le Partage du sensible*. Paris: Éditions La Fabrique, 2000 (64).

*_____. *Aisthesis: Scènes du régime esthétique de l'art*. Paris: Galilée, 2011 (11).

Reimóndez, María. '[Monolingual] Sounds, [No] Translation as Subversion and the Hope for Polyphony' in *The Transnational Story Hub: Between Self And Other*, Ed. by Merlinda Bobis & Belén Martin-Lucas. Barcelona: Centre d'Estudis Australians, U de Barcelona, 2016 (117-139). Web. 21 May 2016.

+_____. *Corpos exorbitantes: Rosalía de Castro, tradutora feminista, en diálogo con Erín Moure*. Santiago: Univ de SdC, 2017.

Van Buren, Peter. 'Walmart Wages Are the Main Reason People Depend on Food Stamps,' *The Nation*, 16 February 2016. Web. 21 May 2016.

Young, Angelo. 'For The First Time Walmart Annual Report Cites Changes To Food Stamps 'And Other Public Assistance Plans' As A Risk Factor,' International Business Times, 24 March 2014. Web. 21 May 2016.

The Book to Come
(an after-affect)

> [...] Rosalía de Castro does not belong to everyone. In the preface to her New Leaves, she makes it clear that she is speaking for the **"people who are missing,"** as Deleuze said, quoting Klee. A people who were not in their time and who had not yet arrived. She spoke for a democracy that's real and not just in the shape of one, a democracy for the precariously employed, for workers and students; she ventured a republic of women no longer defrauded by an "equality" that, however much time passes, never seems to arrive.
> **posted by María do Cebreiro, Galician poet and critic, on 24 February 2019, Rosalía's birthday**

Rosalía de Castro, poet in Galician, began her life in semi-orphanhood, as a child registered to "unknown parents" (they were unmarried, and her father a seminarian, a not uncommon local scandal). She was cared for by relations of her father's then, from five on, lived with her mother. She knew poor health throughout her life, was cash-strapped at times, not poor though she witnessed poverty's desolation. She was a public intellectual, associated alongside her husband with currents of thinking that opposed the complacent accumulative ethos of the conservative bourgeoisie. She was attentive to social relations, to class, to the way capital worked to make some rich and delegitimize others. She worked against systems of exclusion in the world, via language.

New Leaves (1880) was her second book of poetry in Galician, published when she was 43, five years before her death. The book appeared not in the green mountainous NW provinces of Galicia, her home (what in Quebec is called "Espagne Verte"), but across an ocean, on the Caribbean island of Cuba. She had never been in Cuba.

New Leaves can be read across and through (a Deleuzian line of flight that returns) today's global migrations and the reactions to which they have given rise in Europe, across Europe and North Africa/Western Asia, but also in Australia with its offshore detention camps, and at the border between Mexico and the USA, focal point for emigration north from Central America and its unconditioned violences. All are focal points for social conflicts (including those that simmer beneath the administrative surface in the USA and its detention camps) and restiveness resulting from the intersection of climate change (drought in Africa causing movement of peoples) and global flows of capital (oil, arms, minerals, others).

Economic precarity affects women more harshly than it affects men. Everywhere, women are still tasked with the greater part of childcare, care for elders and those with disabilities, and their job mobility is curtailed by their extended role as caregivers. The gender wage gap also means that women must often make do with even less than the average income. Precarity in financial terms leaves more women vulnerable to having to stay in unsafe conditions, i.e. exposed to situations at home, at work, and in the streets where gender violence occurs. All of these consequences of migration and precarity are written into the poetry of Rosalía de Castro. As is poverty as institution, maintained by those who thrive and own... this precarity is visible in our time too.[19]

In the late 19th century, Havana was a colonial hub built on the slave trade and sugar that sustained a mixity of bodies, cultures, ruptures, desires, and many of those bodies were Galicians emigrated from a land that could not provide them a living. De Castro's was a poetry of anger and determination, of what I will call **insistinence**. It raises its voice in favour of the autonomy of women, the poor, the viability of Galician lands, and an economic system that would support its people instead of forcing them to migrate. The right of the poor—or missing people—to be in literature was a force that drove de Castro. She wrote these poems in Galician, in a Galicia whose governments, aristocracy, industrial owners and church spoke Spanish, and whose literati did not encourage work in Galician, let alone work in Galician by a woman.

Rosalía de Castro had never been to Cuba but was not immune to thet mixity of thinking which Caribbean philosopher and poet Édouard Glissant calls "Trembling Thinking": a valiant sense of parts that make a whole (the archipelago), of the unknown and untouchable in each person (opacity), of mixity that results from resistance and struggle (creolization).

---

[19] News sources (Goldstein, Picchi, Van Buren, Young: see readings) have reported on auditors cautioning corporations that cuts to publicly funded food-aid programs could put their profit levels at risk. It seems that minimum-waged workers in the USA at such corporations rely heavily on food stamps to feed their families. Corporations leverage the existence of publicly funded food programs to keep wages low and augment profits.

As some have said, this thinking of Glissant's is an "ethnography of the unknowable", unknowable in the terms of what we "call" knowledge. As well as holding the ineffable, her poetry also holds the heartbreak of the "nous" "autres" "refugiés" of Hannah Arendt, and of the "missing people" of Deleuze. De Castro speaks in harmony with their thinking; as such, she is a poet of the future, whose voice reaches beyond her time.

I see Rosalía de Castro's *New Leaves*, or, here, *In Leaf*, as four books in one, plus a book beyond the book. The title 'Vagaries,'for the first 'book', suggests other words that have been used for women's thinking: 'frivolities,' 'fancies,' 'whimsies.' But de Castro has no intention of writing frivolities. By addressing the Virgin of Paloma, saint of the capital of Spain in her first poem, de Castro stakes out a claim both political (she won't yield to the centre) and anti-patriarchal (no writing about flowers and birds). In the next poem, she rejects the claim that all thoughts have already been thought by men, so there is no use in writing. She then plunges into the material tick-tock of human thinking, praising (Gertrude Stein!) how repetition enables a stable subjectivity. She insists on the movement of a woman's 'I' in the text, on her own thoughts and her own subjectivity. Her work lays a substrate and argument for women's thinking. 'Vagaries' are thoughts, and this first book of twenty poems, each titled using roman numerals in relentless succession[20], elucidates this. She is no melancholy woman of modesty and femininity who is at her best writing personal lyric but a firebrand, one who—as in Rancière—'fictionalizes the real so as to think it.'

De Castro's 'Vagaries' is followed by the book 'Inner Life!,' which offers a poetic thinking of inside and outside, and of their mutually constitutive roles (elaborated thoroughly in our time by philosophers such as Jacques Derrida, Chantal Mouffe, Judith Butler). For de Castro, outside world and inner world interpenetrate. Subjectivity (the intimate) is always political, and constituted through the chance and hazardous relations that constellate communities. As Jacques Rancière says: these political subjects arise and demand transformation in the sensible world.

---

[20]The only poems titled with numbers in the 1880 edition are those of 'Vagaries.' The author's roman numerals, in this book's insistence on thinking, both mark and mock linear logic. In the rest of *New Leaves*, the poems are unnumbered and mostly untitled, rejecting such linearity. The numbers in the first section, and lack thereof in the rest, are potent elements in the structure of the book.

The third book, 'Variations,' holds mostly poems in dialogic form, as call and response, and (instructively and radically) includes listening and silence as dialogic forms.

The fourth book, 'Earthbound,' examines the notion what a home can be and what a society is in which homes do not thrive. The difficulties in Galician homes lead the poet to respond to the Romantic beauty that surrounds them with a declaration of hatred of Romanticism, and, in the final poem of 'Earthbound,' with regret at the brutal intrusion of capital's simulacrae. This last poem, In Leaf's only dated poem, ends with 'March 1880,' the month and year in which de Castro wrote the book's introduction. These two Marches, of introduction and of 'Earthbound''s end, bookend the 4 books of In Leaf.

Yet there is still a book to come, a book apart, lying outside the four-fold time of the main book.

'Twice Widowed' is a book of migrations and migratory effects, primarily on women. As men line up to leave and women are left behind to work, thoughts intensify: the poet examines subjects such as suicide and radical solitude. This is far from the nostalgic resignation attributed to de Castro by earlier critics or by critics who would "normalize" de Castro and Galicia itself as weak and sad! Radical solitude leads Rosalde Castro to face mortality directly, face the breakage of human life wrought by migrations that, in the absence of political change to render homes viable, presents one terrible resolution: the death of subjectivity, as subjects find themselves emigrated (external or internal) outside the gorgeous compass rose of thinking, intimacy, voices, earth.

In creating Rosalía de Castro's work in English, I tried to build a rhythmic soundscape (though rarely rhyming, as do the originals; rhyme is convivial not contrived in Galician) that captures her material sonic texture. I wanted to reflect the variety of spellings, for Galician in the 19th century was not normativized. Part of her poems' modernity and shudder are the very sonorities in her spelling and phrasing, her indents and spacings that help make her poetry different from any other of her time or of ours. Her localisms, aural spellings, Castilian inflections are critical to the materiality of the text: what might seem now as 'deviant' spellings also serve as emotional markings. They are not blemishes but marks of expression. In response, I at times create small 'misspellings' in the English, and enact certain nonstandard punctuations, such as occasionally using the doubled marks for exclamation and question from Spanish, which may also be used in Galician (though today it is also correct to elide the ¿ and the ¡). I also vary words for God, as that vocable resounds differently for a reader in my time. I wanted to make space for a spirituality that admits a wider range of belief, for though she was at least somewhat anti-clerical, de Castro was not pagan. Another word I've altered is 'negro' which I often translate as 'grey' or in other ways rather than translate it as 'black,' since in cotntemporary English, 'black' as a metaphor for negativity occludes a racism that I recognize and banish.

If Rosalía de Castro lived and wrote today in English, I think she'd be C.D. Wright, Myung Mi Kim, Bronwen Wallace, Claudia Rankine, NourbeSe Philip, Dorothy Livesay, Lisa Robertson, Rita Wong, Dionne Brand, Caroline Bergvall, Gwen Benaway, Lindsay Nixon, Divya Victor, Sina Queyras and others. In saying this, I lay claim to Rosalía de Castro as contemporary, as a poet of hybrid displacement, of precarity in the face of capital, and poet of the 'mutation of the sensible' that calls into question the partitions in our world, thus opening other possibilities, other futures. Her art is very much, to borrow a term from Jacques Rancière, French philosopher of aesthetics, a 'mutation in the fabric of the sensible' (*Aisthesis*, 11).

I see and imagine *the missing people* of the present and future for whom the poet wrote. My commentaries/responses are visible in this text, in contrast to the "Galician Classics" English text that appeared in 2016, which, to be consistent with the other volumes of the series and with the shape of translations in general, elided the translator's interferences (though generously allowing some of my spellings). I wanted to create this alternate version for readers because I care, and because this voice of Rosalía de Castro and her fierce intelligence inhabit and transform me. As Jacques Rancière indicates: 'These transformations oblige the modification of the paradigms of art.' (11)

The book is published by me, via Zat-So Productions, because in Official Canada, translating foreign poets receives no publishing support. Rather than emigrate the book, I refuse this exclusionary logic and say, only, citing Elizabeth Bishop's famous poem: ONE ART.

Rosalía de Castro Martínez was born in Santiago de Compostela in 1837. Her mother, María Teresa da Cruz de Castro y Abadía, was of a noble village family from Padrón. Her father, José Martínez Viojo, was a seminarian from the village. Born out of wedlock with a father soon to be a priest, she was whisked away by a family friend or servant from the foundling home where she was born to "unknown parents," into her father's extended family. After an early childhood with her godmother María Francisca Martínez, she joined her mother in Santiago at age 9 or 10, where she was educated as a lady, learning music, drawing, theatre, and French, taking part at events at the Lyceum, a focal point for young artists and writers.

In 1857, a year after moving to Madrid, her first collection of poetry, *La flor* (The Flower) appeared. She was 20. The book was reviewed by writer and historian Manuel Martínez de Murguía, whom she married a year later. They returned to Santiago de Compostela, where in 1859, their first child, Alejandra, was born, and de Castro's first novel, *La hija del mar* (Daughter of the Sea), appeared. Her novel *Flavio* followed in 1861, and a year after her mother died in 1862, Castro published a chapbook of poems, *A mi madre* (To my Mother). In 1863, *Cantares gallegos* (Galician Songs) appeared. Based on forms and motifs from the popular oral tradition, the poems speak of Galician life, in the Galician language. It is a masterpiece of lyric. Her novella *Ruinas* (Ruins) and the article "Las literatas" (Literary Women), on the conditions endured by women writers in 19th century Spain, followed in 1866. In 1867, de Castro's novel *El caballero de las botas azules* (Gentleman in Blue Boots), appeared, a satirical analysis of 19th century Spanish society and of popular novels. Two years later, the family now in Castile, her second child, Aurea, was born. In 1871, the family returned to Galicia, to A Coruña and Santiago de Compostela, following Murguía's job prospects. In Santiago, twins Gala and Ovidio were born in 1872, and a daughter, Amara, in A Coruña in 1874. Adriano, born in 1875, died before the age of two; a seventh child, Valentina, was stillborn in 1877.

In 1880, *Follas novas* (New Leaves), Castro's second collection in Galician, appeared. In its foreword, the poet speaks of her wish to portray the sorrows of those least favoured by Galician society, particularly rural women. The book was revolutionary for its time; Castro she uses her mother tongue as valid not just to portray picturesque scenes of "Green Spain," but to express metaphysical, spiritual, and subjective thinking. Above all, Rosalía and thinking!

El primer loco (First Madman), a look at the Romantic temperament and madness, was Castro's last novel, published in 1881. A year before her death, Castro published her final poetry collection, *En las orillas del Sar* (On the Banks of the River Sar), written in Castilian. It earned Castro acclaim throughout Spain for its innovative experiments with metre, which anticipated modernist poetry. Writers of the Generation of 1898, including Antonio Machado, Juan Ramón Jiménez and Miguel de Unamuno, admired it for its subjective, personal, and existentialist mood. The poems also address contemporary concerns such as ecological destruction: "Los robles" (The Oak Trees) denounces deforestation in Galicia. In the final years of her life, illness sapped de Castro of energy. On July 15, 1885, she died in Padrón of uterine cancer.

The construction of 'Rosalía' as totemic, throughout the late 19th and most of the 20th century, is inseparable from the centralist construction of Galicia as wet, lush, sentimental, its language good for speaking only of landscape and emotion. The radical materiality of de Castro's writing, her feminism and anti-clericalism (not unrelated), were for decades washed over with these constructs, particularly played up under Francoism and in its aftermath (1936-1975 and beyond). Helena Miguélez-Carballeira, in *Galicia, A Sentimental Nation: Genders, Culture and Politics*, offers a lucid analysis of the effects of that discourse on Galician identity. Poet-critic María do Cebreiro, critic Helena González Fernández, and writer-translator María Reimóndez, have published essays that take a more radical and feminist tone: they speak of Rosalía de Castro as rebellious and contemporary, and recognize the multiplicity of her forms, and her many ways of subverting stereotypes regarding women, thinking, poetry, migration, institutionalized poverty, language. In other essays, María do Cebreiro explores the constructs of thinking, irony, shade/shadow, and the infinite in de Castro's work. Critic Olga Castro has written on the (re)canonization of Rosalía de Castro through the optic of translation. María Reimóndez has written on the institutionalization of a nostalgic definition of *morriña*—a longing often attributed to Rosalía de Castro though in *New Leaves* she never mentions it—as both an effect and motor of colonization within Spain itself.[1] Reimóndez has written as well on de Castro as a radical translator. The latest edition of *Follas Novas* in Galician includes extensive critical work by poet, editor, and critic Anxo Angueira which extends the new critical view of Rosalía de Castro as complex and radical in her poetics. *In Leaf* joins their chorus, hoping to bring her anew to readers in English as a poet of modernity, migration, feminism, thinking, mental health.

Erín Moure has published—in Canada, the USA, the UK, variously—over 40 books of poetry, essays, memoir, and translations and co-translations from French, Spanish, Galician, Portuguese, Portunhol and Ukrainian into English. Recent works are *Planetary Noise: Selected Poetry of Erín Moure* (Wesleyan, 2017), *Sitting Shiva on Minto Avenue, by Toots* (New Star, 2017), a translation of Brazilian Wilson Bueno's *Paraguayan Sea* (Nightboat, 2017), and a reissue with introduction by Sonnet L'Abbé of *Furious* (Anansi, 1988). Her latest works in 2019 are a translation of Lupe Gómez, *Camouflage* (Circumference Books) from Galician, a co-traduction with Roman Ivashkiv of Yuri Izdryk, *Smokes* (Lost Horse Press) from Ukrainian, and her own *The Elements* (Anansi). She is currently preparing book-length translations of books by Galician poets Chus Pato, *The Face of the Quartzes*, and Uxío Novoneyra; *The Uplands: Book of the Courel* (forthcoming 2020 from Veliz Books); as well as translations from the Spanish of Chilean poet Andrés Ajens, *So-Lair Storm*, and 10 "translations" of John Wendell by Argentinian poet Juan Gelman (forthcoming 2020, Eulalia Press.) Moure holds two honorary doctorates from universities in Canada and Spain, was 2017 Creative Fellow at the Woodberry Poetry Room at Harvard University, and in November 2019 will be International Translator in Residence at The Queen's College, Oxford University, UK. She lives in Montreal.

Some Good Company for RdC (+One Title by Each)

Avasilichioaei, Oana. *Eight-Track*.
Bachmann, Ingeborg. *Darkness Spoken*. Tr. Peter Filkins
Benaway, Gwen. *Holy Wild*.
Bergvall, Caroline. *Drift*.
Brand, Dionne. *Ossuaries*.
Brossard, Nicole. *White Piano*. Tr. Robert Majzels and EM.
Carr, Angela. *The Rose Concordance*.
Cole, Norma. *Where Shadows Will*.
Eng, Mercedes. *Prison Industrial Complex Explodes*.
Fong, Nicole Raziya. *Perfact*.
Gómez, Lupe. *Camouflage*. Tr. EM.
Howe, Susan. *Debths*.
Kim, Myung Mi. *The Commons*.
Lalonde, Catherine. *The Faerie Devouring*. Tr. Oana Avasilichioaei.
Livesay, Dorothy. *The Unquiet Bed*.
Neveu, Chantal. *A Spectacular Influence*. Tr. Nathanaël.
Nicholson, Cecily. *Wayside Sang*.
Nixon, Lindsay. *Nîtisânak*. (memoir)
Pato, Chus. *Flesh of Leviathan*. Tr. EM.
Philip, NourbeSe. *Zong*.
Queyras, Sina. *My Ariel*.
Rankine, Claudia. *Don't Let Me Be Lonely*.
Robertson, Lisa. *The Men*.
Sze, Gillian. *Panicle*.
Vermette, Katherena. *North End Love Songs*.
Victor, Divya. *Kith*.
Wallace, Bronwen. *Common Magic*.
Wolf, Uljana. *Subsisters*. Tr. Sophie Seita
Wong, Rita. *Sybil Unrest*. With Larissa Lai.
Wright, C.D. *Rising, Falling, Hovering*.
Zisimatos, Eleni. *Nearly Terminal*.
+
Agamben, Giorgio. *L'Usage des corps*. Tr. Joël Gayraud.
Collis, Stephen. *The Commons*.
Hall, Phil. *White Porcupine*.
Kellough, Kaie. *Magnetic Equator*.
Majzels, Robert. *Kharlamov's Ankle*.

www.ingramcontent.com/pod-product-compliance
Lightning Source LLC
Chambersburg PA
CBHW051821090426
42736CB00011B/1591